C000022509

We Welcome You

Baptism Preparation
with Families

We Welcome You

Baptism Preparation with Families

Jacqui Hyde
with Sandra Millar & Paul Butler

THE CHURCH
OF ENGLAND

© Jacqui Hyde, Sandra Millar & Paul Butler 2016

Church House Publishing
Church House
Great Smith Street
London SW1P 3AZ

Published 2016 by Church House Publishing

Second impression 2018

All rights reserved. No part of this publication may be reproduced or stored or transmitted by any means or in any form, electronic or mechanical, including photocopying, recording, or any information storage and retrieval system without written permission, which should be sought from the Copyright Administrator, Church House Publishing, Church House, Great Smith Street, London SW1P 3AZ.

Email: copyright@churchofengland.org

The Authors have asserted their right under the Copyright, Designs and Patents Act 1988, to be identified as the Authors of this Work.

The opinions expressed in this book are those of the authors and do not necessarily reflect the official policy of the General Synod or the Archbishops' Council of the Church of England.

British Library Cataloguing in Publication Data

A catalogue record for this book is available from the British Library

ISBN 978 0 7151 47221

Printed and bound in Great Britain by Ashford Colour Press Ltd.

CONTENTS

INTRODUCTION:
FOR THE DAY OR FOR LIFE?

Sandra Millar

———

I can still remember my first ever pre-baptism preparation visit. I was a curate in the kind of church where the focus for baptism prep was a home visit by the minister, who talked through the service with added theological explanation. After that, the family were put in touch with a baptism visitor, usually an older mum, who would be there at the service and would get in touch with the family before the big day.

This visit was largely led by a grandmother, although the mum was also present. The baby made a late appearance with the father (something that I have noticed is quite common: fathers seem to have to go out when the vicar arrives and make a sudden reappearance just as they are about to step out the front door). I talked them through the service with the zeal and passion that the newly ordained bring to such situations. The questions were nearly all of a practical nature, about where to stand and what to do, with a bit of a worry about whether they had to say much. The highlight of the visit was when I was asked if I would bless a necklace – it was a family tradition to give a new child some jewellery. I am not sure how well I explained the significance of baptism, and I don't know whether or not the child or the family have yet engaged fully with the Christian faith. But I prayed for them then and I pray for them now ... and I hope the necklace still reminds them of a really special day.

So much baptism preparation feels disappointing. We come away not sure whether we have said anything meaningful or not, and this can only add to a diffidence or ambivalence about the real significance of the event to the family. It can take a lot of time and resource, whether visiting one family or organizing a series of meetings.

As part of the recent Archbishops' Council-funded work surrounding the baptism of children under twelve, major research has been done with both clergy and families. This research has explored a wide range of issues around baptism and how parents experience it, and it has helped to shape the way this course has been devised. The research revealed some surprising and some less surprising things about baptism preparation and how it impacts parents.

Alongside the research with families, conversations were also held with around 300 clergy in a series of discussion groups, and it really wasn't a surprise to find that many of them found baptism preparation difficult. Some churches decide to set the barrier high, asking parents to come on lengthy courses, perhaps attending Alpha or a similar programme, in the hope that this helps them to have a proper appreciation of all that they are promising. Many have a home visit along the lines I describe above, which is an intensive use of time and may or may not have any real impact on understanding. For some families having a home visit from the vicar may feel intimidating – it's clear a lot of tidying up goes on beforehand in some households! However baptism preparation is offered, for many there was a real sense of anxiety about whether or not preparation was effective. Many clergy worry about whether parents have understood what they are doing with and for their child, and underlying that is a fear that they don't really mean what they say.

This emphasis on intellectual understanding may be rooted in the way we are trained as ministers; regardless of our own educational and socio-economic background, qualifications of at least degree level are now expected to be attained. Perhaps it is even further rooted in the past, back to the days when the church was often the main location for academic knowledge, and theology was 'the queen of the sciences'. Consciously or unconsciously, we expect those who indicate an interest in faith, however tentatively or casually, to also have some level of understanding. Traditionally, adults and children preparing for baptism undertook 'catechesis' – a period of religious education – and would have been examined as to the extent of their knowledge.

Canon law still requires us to prepare candidates for baptism, but does not specify the type or form that it should take. So as part of the research carried out in 2013, we not only explored how families felt about baptism and how they experienced the service, we also asked about the kind of preparation they had received. Eighty per cent said that preparation involved a 'chat with the vicar' while 23 per cent had attended a short course; however, less than a quarter thought that the church insisted on it. So when we had the research back from the thousand families that were interviewed we expected there might be evidence of a lack of understanding, and perhaps a sense that the parents felt unprepared and uninformed. But this is when the surprises began.

Families were asked in a number of different ways if they felt prepared or ready for their child's christening. Nearly 60 per cent said they felt well prepared and understood what was going to happen, that they understood the significance and knew what their responsibilities would be. However, it emerged that for most parents this is more to do with knowing what is expected of them on the day than realizing that baptism is the beginning of a life-long journey.

'Before we got married, we had marriage preparation, and I think my husband went to a sort of get ready for christening meeting, which I wish I would have gone to because men don't really relay things very well. I don't think you get the same kind of support in preparing a christening as you do with getting married. And yes, you probably go through the nuts and bolts of it. But I'm not sure there's enough about why you were doing it and the reasons ... I'm not sure you are given more of context and the bigger picture.'

'There was very little prior input from the church other than a group "admin" meeting in which a brief explanation of the significance of baptism was explained, along with the format of the service.'

It is very important for parents to feel comfortable with the mechanics of the day. For many families church and church practice has become unfamiliar (or is even completely unknown), and for others the christening day itself is stressful to organize and prepare. This was reinforced when we asked parents about the day itself and whether they had any anxieties. Very few had real anxieties about the day, with only 7 per cent saying they were uneasy, embarrassed or uncomfortable with the words of the promise, and an even smaller 4 per cent saying they were unsure of the meaning of the service. The biggest fears that parents voiced were around being socially visible, with 16 per cent worried about singing and 13 per cent expressing unease about standing at the front. By far the biggest anxiety was about their own or other children being naughty or noisy. It seems that baptism preparation as experienced by many families helps them feel at ease with the practicalities of the day. There is a marked contrast between clergy worries about understanding and meaning and the parents' sense that they have been prepared for this day.

However, there is also a sense from the parents of expecting something more from the preparation: although they wanted to feel confident about the mechanics of the day, they also felt that there could be something else to be explored. The programme of baptism preparation presented here is about trying to go a bit deeper and address some of these issues, meeting parents at their point of understanding and helping them to discover more of God's great love for them and all it could mean.

Most parents are seriously motivated about asking for a christening for their child. After all, it is no longer the social norm. Today, fewer than one in six families choose to have a child baptized in the Church of England. Some may have a thanksgiving, but many more don't any longer feel the need to mark the arrival of a child with any specific ritual, although there may be plenty of family parties and other gatherings to celebrate. If high street merchandise is anything to go by (and it often is an indicator of trends), 'baby showers' are becoming more and more popular. In the year 2000 I went to my first ever 'baby shower' – in San Francisco. I had never really heard of such a thing outside of a movie or two. But in the past few years I have been to more than a handful among family and friends. The 'baby shower' clearly provides an occasion to get together, predominantly with girlfriends and family to celebrate the coming child.

Increasingly parents are choosing to have a child baptized a little later, with 35 per cent of baptisms for children aged between one and twelve. Closer analysis of this in the parishes where we piloted the new christening resources showed that of those 35 per cent, three-quarters were aged between one and four. Anecdotally, many clergy observe that baptisms often happen around a first birthday, or sometimes for two or more children at once, with a sense that the family is now complete. The family may have been thinking about a christening for some time, deciding about godparents even before a child is born, but postponing it until there is a moment when friends and relatives from far and wide can get together. It may also be that the growth in pre-birth celebrations means that waiting a while before another celebration is both practical and realistic.

The research showed clearly that whenever they make that decision, families clearly call the occasion a christening – and the new Church of England website and print materials all reflect this (**www.churchofenglandchristenings.org**). Once the decision is made families will look for christening cakes and gowns and gifts and cards – and the word is widely used in the media to describe the event. However, the church service is called a baptism service – and baptism is what is happening. So on the website and in other resources the word 'baptism' is introduced early on, and one of the first pre-preparation tasks is to explain to parents, even at the initial contact, that 'during the christening your baby will be baptized, just as during a wedding a couple are married'.

WHY DO PARENTS ASK FOR A CHRISTENING?

Parents want their child to have the best start in life and to make good choices as they go through life. It is this that is often behind the request for a christening. The research shows that parents are often on a journey of faith themselves, one that goes right back to their own positive experiences of Sunday school, youth group, church school or even parade services as part of belonging to a uniformed organization. One father talked about the awe he felt at big parade services in the local cathedral, reflecting on moments of wonder and amazement – 'I want my child to have that as well,' he said. Faith journeys are long, and not always church journeys, but when a family asks for a christening there is an opportunity to discover something of that journey.

Parenthood also brings both responsibility and vulnerability. Parents in our research were acutely aware of a shift in feelings after the birth of a child, often particularly expressed by dads: 'It's the most amazing feeling, not like anything else you will ever feel,' said one. With that awareness comes a heightened sense of what could go wrong for their child, the possibility of harm befalling them or being caught up in the wrong in the world. I have always found it easy to get parents to name the sins and bad choices that they fear their child might fall into – drugs and gangs come high on the list, even in the heartlands of rural England! Parents may express this in a desire for protection and blessing, but also in language about making right choices in the future, seeing a baptism as a key part of helping to make this happen.

The sense that a christening will be part of helping a child to make good choices later in life is strongly expressed in the research. Parents are still very positive about what some may call 'the ethics and values of the church', sensing that the moral framework of the Christian faith is a valuable part of a child's life. Part of preparing families for baptism may be about exploring what some of these values and ethics might be, and how they see them lived out in their day-to-day family life.

For some parents – and godparents – the baptism of a child is a key milestone on their own spiritual journey. It can be a moment when their own thoughts, feelings and questions come to the forefront and something in the conversations or in the service itself fans a spark into life. On several occasions recently when presenting this research to diocesan clergy and lay people, someone has come up to me with just such a story. Someone recently ordained shared with me how the feelings he had when his daughter was baptized stirred a response that led to his Christian faith springing to life. He clearly recalls feeling called to ordination right there in the baptism service! So the opportunity to engage with parents where they are on their journey is an important part of talking through baptism.

Above all, baptism is about people. For new parents it is about their present family and friends, but also about their family across generations. It is not just about connecting to the place where they currently live, but also about reaching back to the story of parents and grandparents and becoming part of a bigger story. Inviting guests to share with them in both the church service and the party helps celebrate community and family life. The baptism service is about welcoming a child into the community of God's people, giving them a place where they will always belong and becoming part of the world-wide church across time and place. Making connections between the experience of human family and that of the family of fellow travellers on the journey of faith is also a valuable part of preparing for baptism.

The baptism service itself, whether held separately or integrated into Sunday worship, is rich in symbolism, symbols that make an impact on those who bring a child to be baptized. Parents find the candle and the water to be deeply significant, and are moved by moments when their child is mentioned by name in prayers and blessing. They may not always be able to articulate the complex layers of theological meaning that underpin the symbols, but they sense that something special and significant happens. Baptism preparation is an opportunity to help parents become aware of the symbols of the service itself, and also to raise their own thoughts and responses.

DEVELOPING THE RESOURCES

Over the course of a year, 150 parishes tested out a range of printed resources designed to help parents and godparents find out more about christening. The resources are supported by a website for parents, godparents and guests **www.churchofenglandchristenings.org** (more information about all the resources can be found at **www.churchsupporthub.org**). Clergy from these parishes attended a 24-hour conference to explore the research findings and as a result changed some of their language and approaches to baptism. One of the most significant impacts felt by parishes during that year was the shift they felt happened in parents' understanding of baptism. Ninety-three per cent felt that parents were now realizing that baptism was the start of something rather than an end in itself. The journey imagery is used repeatedly in both publicity information and in this course to reinforce this message, one taken from the introduction to Pastoral Services.[1]

---

[1] *Common Worship: Pastoral Services*, Church House Publishing, 2000, p. 3.

This course has been developed to reflect some of the insights of the research. It takes seriously parents' desire to have their child christened, and works at understanding and building bridges between their language and motivation and the language and meaning of the church. It also aims to be flexible, so that for those who can or want to offer a three-week programme of preparation there is ample material. Should a church wish to run a longer course to help parents think about faith in the context of baptism, there is a lot of additional material so that the programme can be expanded.

But the material is also realistic and practical, recognizing that for many churches a single session is going to work best. At the end of the book are two programmes for a single preparation session, one with multiple families, and one with a single family, perhaps at home. However, the research clearly showed that meeting other families and people other than the vicar is a key factor in whether or not families continue to have an ongoing relationship with the church. Even those families who are having a child baptized in a church that is not in the community where they live will benefit from an opportunity to meet the wider congregation: the broader the welcome, the more positive the experience, the more likely they are to go along to their local church. Although it may not be practical to meet a family who live further afield, the wonders of technology might allow for a conversation via Skype.

After the service, the research indicates that parents really value hearing from the church again. Almost every organization we get involved with in life – from the gym to the toy shop – keeps in touch through regular emails. Even if your church can't do that, don't be afraid to send parents information that offers a warm welcome to the activities and worship at your church. Include information about the social and community happenings you are either leading or taking part in – events such as a summer fete are ideal for families to attend. Even if families come along to only two or three events over the course of a year, they are maintaining contact.

Alongside this, practical suggestions for prayers, relevant Bible stories and other resources to help children grow in faith are welcomed. A baptism is the beginning of a journey for the family and for the church that accompanies them, so the time taken preparing well and keeping them company is time that can help them grow in the knowledge and love of God, and of his Son, Jesus Christ.

HOW TO USE THIS BOOK

The core of this book is a baptism preparation course designed to take three sessions of approximately 90 minutes – but it is very flexible so can be shortened or lengthened. Take time to become familiar with the material and find those people in church who will be comfortable using this kind of creative approach as well as those who are warm and welcoming. This material does not have to be led by a vicar, although it is great if the minister who will conduct the baptism is present some of the time.

RUNNING A SHORT 3-WEEK PROGRAMME

Plan the dates – you could run Sessions 1 and 3 and then use Session 2 as a rehearsal or perhaps use Session 3 as a follow-up after the event (which does of course run the risk of the families having lost interest, depending on how well they have built friendships and connections).

Send invitations – make sure parents are informed and know who to reply to and what to expect. Special baptism preparation invitations are available on **www.churchprinthub.org** if you would find them useful, and **www.pastoralservicesdiary.org** can help with managing reminders and contacts.

Prepare well – check through the material and the resources needed, making sure all that is needed is ready. Check the space and the provision of good refreshments – hospitality really matters.

You will also need to photocopy any handouts for the session. Alternatively you can download these from **www.churchsupporthub.org**.

Keep in contact during the course – send text reminders or create a Facebook group. This can be really helpful and can create a sense of community among those attending.

EXTENDING THE COURSE

If you would like to make this a longer programme, look through each week carefully and use the additional activities to create further sessions. For example, you might decide to run six one-hour sessions, spreading each part over two weeks. There are lots of permutations.

SHORTENING THE COURSE

A suggested one-session programme has been included: this might also be supported with a very practical rehearsal in church.

BUILDING FAITH

Remember that parents and godparents are themselves on a journey of faith that may stretch over many years. They may have widely differing experiences of church and of the story of Jesus. The activities can be adapted to encourage and support parents and godparents in their own understanding of faith, and time may need to be taken to answer questions and share something of the life of Jesus.

Enjoy the journey!

BAPTISM: WHAT IS IT ALL ABOUT?
PAUL BUTLER

'We acknowledge one baptism for the forgiveness of sins.'

Yes, Anglicans believe in baptism. Unlike the other dominical sacrament, the Lord's Supper, it is even included in the Nicene Creed. So it clearly matters a great deal. We believe that baptism is very important. But just what about it do we believe, and why? What do those who bring their infants, or present themselves, for baptism believe about it today? The reasons they give are clear. Baptism is about thankfulness for life; it is about loving the child and wanting the best for them. It is about belonging to a family and perhaps to something bigger than the family. It is about values and morals. It is about wanting light rather than darkness. It is about life and hope. It is thus an enormous opportunity to connect people with the good news of Jesus. It creates an awesome responsibility on the part of the church to care for such parents and children well, not seeing the baptism as the end of contact but as a significant first major step. It is about helping the family grow in their experience and knowledge of God's love.

According to the Catechism in the Book of Common Prayer, a sacrament is 'an outward and visible sign of an inward and spiritual grace given unto us, ordained by Christ himself, as a means whereby we receive the same, and a pledge to assure us thereof'. So we believe in baptism first of all because of Jesus Christ's command to his disciples. We practise it because Jesus commanded us to do so. It is a sign of something that is happening inside us. But it is not simply a sign; in some way the very act of baptism affects that which it signifies.

That might all be starting to sound a little complicated, so let's try and unpack it. We will begin with baptism as given to us by Jesus himself.

JESUS AND BAPTISM

Jesus was himself baptized by John the Baptizer (Matthew 3.13–17; Mark 1.9–11; Luke 3.21–22; John 1.29–34). John was Jesus' cousin, raised by his parents knowing that he had a special calling from God (Luke 1). John began a public ministry which from the outset involved baptism (Luke 3.1–3). It appears that John took a practice that was well known to the Jews of his day and revolutionized it. The Jews were used to the idea that if a Gentile wished to become a member of the Jewish community they had to go through a ritual washing, and for the men, circumcision. The ritual washing symbolized the need for cleansing from sin before becoming a member of the people of God.

John's revolution was that he offered this ritual washing to Jews. He understood that the purpose of his preaching was to prepare the way for the coming of the Messiah, for which the people needed to get ready. This readiness involved a recognition of the sinfulness of the individual and of the nation of Israel. John's water baptism was 'of repentance for the forgiveness of sins' (Luke 3.3; Matthew 3.6, 11; Mark 1.4). It is a cleansing act that must then be lived out in holy lives (Matthew 3.7ff; Luke 3.7ff). It is to this baptism that Jesus comes from Nazareth in Galilee and submits himself. According to Matthew's account, John does not think Jesus should be baptized (Matthew 3.14) but yields to Jesus' greater wisdom of seeing this as an act of obedience. It is in, and at, his baptism that Jesus receives the testimony of God both in the descent of the Holy Spirit and in the voice from heaven declaring, 'This is my beloved Son, with whom I am well pleased' (Matthew 3.13–17; Mark 1.9–11; Luke 3.21–22; John 1.32–34).

John continued to baptize people after he had recognized in Jesus the arrival of the Messiah. He also started to point people towards Jesus as being the one whom God had promised, who would baptize with the Spirit (John 1.29–36). But John knew his time was drawing to a close and before long he was arrested and ultimately killed by Herod.

While John had a ministry of baptism, he was not the only person to do so at this time. As we read in the Gospel of the apostle John, the disciples of Jesus also conducted baptisms (John 3.22–4.2). We know nothing of this practice from the Synoptic Gospels but the implication is that from the very outset of his public ministry Jesus commanded his disciples to baptize new followers. Given the clear ordinance to baptize after the resurrection, and the practice of the early church, what we read about in Acts was a continuation of an existing practice rather than something entirely new.

Now the command to baptize is not found in either of Luke's commissions to the disciples (Luke 24.44–53; Acts 1), nor in John. It is there in the longer ending of Mark (Mark 16.16), although not as a command. It is only firmly found in Matthew 28.19. Here the command is clear, to baptize 'in the name of the Father and of the Son and of the Holy Spirit'. Some argue that this trinitarian formula was an innovation of the early church rather than being based on the words of Jesus himself, given that the formula used for baptism in Acts is consistently baptism in the name of Jesus, Jesus Christ or Lord Jesus (Acts 2.38; 10.48; 19.5). Personally, I am content to accept these words as those of the risen Jesus, given Jesus' own reference to God as his Father, his recognition of himself as Son (of Man) and his promise of the Holy Spirit. But either way, it is inarguable that the risen Jesus commanded his disciples to baptize.

Yet despite the fact that there is only this one clear instance of Jesus' ordinance to baptize, the formularies of the church have always declared that baptism is done because Jesus commanded the church to do so. This is because it is also based on the evidence, found in the book of Acts and the New Testament letters, of what the apostles, and the wider early church, actually did. Let's now consider this in greater detail.

THE EARLY CHURCH AND BAPTISM

The story of the day of Pentecost makes it abundantly clear that right from the start the church saw baptism as the sign of conversion to Jesus as Messiah and Lord. It was a sign of repentance for the forgiveness of sins, so it was similar to John's baptism, but also connected with the gift of the Spirit and so associated with John's promise of the coming Messiah. This baptism also was 'in the name of Jesus Christ' (Messiah in Hebrew) (Acts 2.37ff). Baptism is clearly, then, the mark of entry into the church.

Many instances follow as the story of Acts unfolds. Philip baptized the Samaritans as a sign of their belief in the kingdom of God and the name of Jesus Christ (Acts 8.12f). In his encounter with the Ethiopian court official it is very clear that baptism was part of Philip's explanation of the good news of Jesus because the Ethiopian requests baptism and Philip enacts it (Acts 8.26–40). As we all know, Saul, the great persecutor of the church, is met by Christ on the road to Damascus, and is blinded. After his sight is restored, he is immediately baptized. He knew that baptism had to follow his decision to submit to Jesus as Lord (Acts 9.18).

Peter is very quick to baptize Cornelius and his household after the Spirit has descended upon them all. For Peter, baptism is the logical thing to do following this gift of the Spirit (Acts 10.47–48). Likewise, Paul rapidly baptizes the Philippian jailer and his household (Acts 16.33).

As discussed earlier, there may be only one clearly recorded command of the risen Jesus to baptize, but it is abundantly clear from these passages that the early church saw baptism as an essential part of how people expressed their faith in Jesus as Lord and Christ and entered into the life of this new church.

The New Testament letters endorse this view further and we will look at them soon.

But before leaving Acts, a quick point about how this baptism was clearly seen as quite distinctive from that of John the Baptist. The story of Apollos in Acts tells us that while he 'taught accurately the things concerning Jesus, knew only the baptism of John' (Acts 18.25). So 'the way of God' is explained to him more accurately by Priscilla and Aquila; the implication clearly is that part of this was about Jesus and baptism. This is followed up by Luke with the story of the Ephesian disciples who had been baptized 'into John's baptism' (Acts 19.3). Paul tells them about Jesus and, significantly, then baptizes them 'in the name of the Lord Jesus' and prays for them to receive the Holy Spirit (Acts 19.1–7).

What seems abundantly clear from these two accounts is that Christian baptism was seen as clearly distinctive because of in whose name the baptism took place, and also because of its connection with Jesus as the one who baptizes in the Spirit. Water baptism and Spirit baptism are thus connected in some way in the mind and practice of the early church. They are not synonymous, as there is separate prayer and experience, but as with Cornelius and Saul there is a connection. This too is picked up in the letters.

But before turning to the letters to explore more about the understanding of baptism, let us ask the question of who was baptized in the early church, in the light of who we might consider to be eligible for baptism today.

BAPTISM FOR WHOM?

It is clear that very large numbers of those baptized in Acts were adults. These included adult Jews who had come to believe that Jesus was the crucified and risen Messiah, and adult Gentiles who had come to believe that this Jewish Messiah was indeed the Lord of all and that his death and resurrection was for them too.

As we have seen, this was a baptism of repentance – a turning away from sin towards God, a change of mind and orientation of life. It was a baptism for the forgiveness of sins – those baptized believed that in Jesus forgiveness was given to them.

These believers were joining themselves to Jesus Christ, for baptism was 'in the name of the Lord Jesus'. Thus it was also an act of joining the community of Christ, of belonging. It is important to remember always that baptism is into Christ, not into the church. By being baptized into Christ, we become part of Christ's people, but the order is important.

It was also an act of being baptized into and with the Holy Spirit. Jesus' distinctive baptism is 'with, or into, the Holy Spirit', for in one sense anyone can baptize into or with water but Jesus alone is able to baptize with the Spirit. The gift of the Spirit can only by given by God, and by none other. But was it only adults who were baptized in the early church?

Here I think we have to take the Jewish background of the first Christians deeply seriously. They were imbued with a conviction that every male child should be circumcised on the eighth day to show that they belonged to the covenant people of God. This was never delayed. It was never suggested that waiting until the child could choose for himself was an option. Every child belonged, and the mark of belonging should therefore be given. This connection of baptism with circumcision emerges in Romans 2 and Colossians 2.11; for while Paul recognized that circumcision could be a merely physical act whose significance might then be ignored, forgotten or even abandoned, he also knew that it mattered as a sign of God's covenant. Given this deep-rooted background of circumcision and inclusion it seems logical to conclude that the apostles would apply the sign of the new covenant in the same way. They would have baptized the children of those adults coming for baptism.

To this I believe we have to add Jesus' own approach and attitude to children, including babes in arms. He welcomed them and was furious with the disciples when they tried to stop parents bringing small children to him for his blessing

(Matthew 18.1–14; 19.13–15; Mark 9.33–37, 42-50; 10.13–16; Luke 18.15–17). At every turn, Jesus welcomed children and recognized that the kingdom belongs to them.

Given Jesus' attitude to children, and the background of the circumcision of Jewish boys, it seems quite inconceivable that the first Jewish converts did not bring their children for baptism and that the apostles would not have baptized them. While the reference to 'children' in Acts 2.39 cannot be understood definitively as referring to children there at the time, its natural sense is that children are included.

Further evidence is to be found in the accounts of the household baptisms of Cornelius, the Philippian jailer and Stephanas (1 Corinthians 1.16). Neither of these explicitly mention children but it seems highly unlikely that they would have been excluded from such baptisms. Paul's addresses to children in Ephesians 6.1–3 and Colossians 3.20 also imply that they are members of the church (and therefore baptized).

When we add to this the evidence of the baptism of infants and children in the writings from just after the apostolic era, then it does appear legitimate to conclude that from the very outset infants and children were baptized in the early church. Certainly, this would have been the children of new Christian families. When Christians were such a minority in the population it was bound to be confined to this group alone.

So should baptism be confined solely to the children of Christians today, or in a very different era is it legitimate to offer baptism to infants and children whose parents may be less obviously believers?

Before exploring this, let us go back to the Scriptures and take a look at the letters. Just what do they tell us about baptism?

WHAT DOES BAPTISM SIGNIFY AND SEAL?

Death, burial and resurrection – Romans 6, Colossians 2.12ff

It is widely accepted that the dominant symbolism of baptism in the New Testament letters is that of death, burial and resurrection. As Jesus died for us all so the believer dies with Christ, is buried with him and is raised with him (Galatians 2.20; 2 Corinthians 5.14–17). Romans 6 is Paul's fullest explanation of baptism in these terms, and it is clear too in Colossians 2. This death, burial and resurrection is symbolized by going down into the waters, being immersed and then brought up again.

Here it is important to note that baptism is never self-administered — it is always done to the person. Christ died for us; we died with him. Christ was raised from death; we are raised with him. He has done it for us, so being baptized by another visibly reminds us that we cannot save ourselves — it is an act of God by the Spirit.

So full immersion baptism, as supported in the Book of Common Prayer, symbolizes this best. This is also why, in the Orthodox tradition, babies are completely immersed in water. I think there is a strong case for finding ways of baptizing adults by immersion where possible. Using a local river, lake, the sea or even a mini indoor collapsible pool all work.

There is also a case for following the Orthodox example of immersing babies but not many Church of England fonts are deep enough!

In Christ we pass from death into life. We are a new creation.

The giving of the candle in a baptism service also symbolizes this. Our liturgical language tends to emphasize the thought of passing from darkness into light. But in many churches, the candle given at baptism is lit from the Paschal/Easter candle. Therefore, this candle also symbolizes Christ's bursting through death for us. It is alight to remind us that Jesus is alive, risen. So the giving of the candle stands as a symbol of the new life and light God has given us in Christ.

WASHED

Acts 22.16; 1 Corinthians 6.11; Ephesians 5.26; Titus 3.5;
Hebrews 10.22; 1 Peter 3.21; John 3.5; 13.13.8; 1 John 5.6ff

While dying and rising is the dominant imagery associated with baptism in the New Testament letters, there are other key images. John the Baptist's forgiveness of sins was a washing away of them, in order for people to be clean and prepared for the Messiah. The forgiveness of sins in Jesus is also a washing away of sin. This is arguably best symbolized in the pouring of water over someone. As is suggested in *Common Worship*, 'the use of a substantial amount of water is desirable' (*Initiation Services*, p. 336). Sprinkling with water can also be understood in this way (Hebrews 10.22) but the use of a substantial amount in immersion or pouring emphasizes the symbolism more fully.

CLOTHED

Galatians 3.27; Ephesians 4.24; Colossians 3.5ff; Romans 13.14

Being in Christ is also described in the New Testament letters as being 'clothed with Christ'. In Colossians, it is preceded by the image of putting off the old self. The turning away from sin and turning to Christ is like divesting ourselves of an old set of clothing and donning a new one. It is this imagery that led to the development, in the fourth or fifth century, of the use of a change of clothing at baptisms. One set of clothes would be worn before entering the water and a new robe would be placed on the newly baptized as they came out of the water; this new robe was often bleached white. In time, this developed into the tradition of christening gowns and the simple wearing of white for the ceremony. It remains worthwhile considering the significance of clothing worn for baptism.

SPIRIT BAPTIZED

1 Corinthians 12.13; Romans 8; Galatians 3.1-4.6

We have already noted the significance of Jesus being the Spirit baptizer and the apparent connection between water and Spirit baptism as the story of the early church unfolds in Acts. The life of the Spirit is unfolded in depth in chapters such as Romans 8, 1 Corinthians 12, Galatians 3–5 and Ephesians 4. Water baptism is clearly understood as signifying the outpouring of the Spirit.

This is closely connected, too, with the whole idea of being adopted into God's family; of being children and heirs of God in Christ; of belonging to Christ's family, and body. This is the new life of the Spirit, which is seen in Spirit-empowered living in which the Spirit's gifts are exercised.

Pouring water would seem to signify this outpouring of the Spirit best. Alongside this, the use of oil developed in the post-apostolic early church as a symbol of the Spirit. If anointing takes place after the baptism, it expresses the richness of the gift of the Spirit. This clearly makes symbolic sense, although care should always be taken that any signing or anointing with oil is not confused with the act of baptism itself.

These images interact and feed off one another. Within the short letter of Colossians we have death and resurrection; we have the divesting and donning of clothing. In Titus 3.5, we have both washing and renewing of the Spirit.

But in all images, the baptism has to be lived out. Baptism into Christ is clearly seen as a once-and-for-all act, mirroring the once-and-for-all nature of Christ's death on the cross. However, it clearly requires a lifetime of being lived out. The baptized are expected to live differently – they are to live the way of Christ Jesus. Baptism commits the person to a life of following Jesus.

Next, we return to the question of who should be eligible for baptism today.

BAPTISM TODAY

If baptism is the sign and symbol of dying and rising with Christ, of being washed clean from sin, of being gifted with the Spirit and adopted into God's family, then for whom is it applicable today?

In the early church, it would seem that baptism was for adults who had made a conscious decision to place themselves into Christ and the Christian community. It was a decisive act that broke with the past and set a course for the future. The infants and children of such adults, and the slaves of the more well-to-do families, were incorporated into this and would have been baptized.

But with Christendom came a more general and, in a sense, indiscriminate baptism. The whole population was considered to be part of the Church. Nonconformists showed their dissent by not baptizing their children, but keeping it as an act for later childhood or adulthood.

We now live in a culture that many believe to be both post-Christian and post-Christendom, and yet much of the heritage of Christendom remains. The Church of England is still established by law. The Queen is still its supreme governor. Church of England bishops still sit in the House of Lords as Lords Spiritual. The local parish church in vast numbers of communities is still loved, wanted and valued, even if not often used. A high percentage of marriages and funerals are still conducted in Anglican churches. A quarter of schools are Church of England schools.

In this setting, in some areas large numbers still bring their children to be christened; in other areas this is much less the case. We have, I believe, moved beyond the place where most people bringing their children for baptism simply want them 'done'. The research behind the Baptism Project, cited throughout this book, backs this up. For those bringing children to be christened today, there is a seriousness in it, even if that might be unclear in content.

In this setting, we want to offer welcome to the kingdom, as Jesus did to those who felt outcast. We want to welcome infants and children in the same way that Jesus did; we have no desire to turn them or their parents away, because we seek to follow our Lord's example.

So in this post-Christendom era, does baptism express that welcome? I believe it does. However unclear or tentative the faith of the parents may be in bringing their child for baptism, they are nonetheless expressing some awareness of their need for God's help. They are expressing thankfulness for the life of their child. They want the very best for their child and somehow recognize that God, and the church, might well want that as well. By welcoming and helping parents and godparents think more about this, we set the child on the way of Christ. If we turn them away we give a very clear message that we do not value their tentative faith; we do not value the child. It is most likely we will never see those parents again and they will raise their child with a negative view of the church and thus of Christ.

In our post-Christendom era, what do people really think baptism is about? We have to recognize that it is usually not initially about death and resurrection, or about washing from sin or adoption into the life of the Spirit. It is about thankfulness for life; it is about loving the child and wanting the best for her or him. It is about belonging to a family and perhaps to something bigger than the family. It is about values and morals. It is about wanting light rather than darkness. It is about life and hope. It is thus an enormous opportunity to connect people with the good news of Jesus. It creates an awesome responsibility on the part of the church to care for such parents and children well, not seeing the baptism as the end of contact but a significant first major step. It is about helping the family grow in their experience and knowledge of God's love.

It also makes admission to communion and confirmation very important in subsequent years – but those are not the subject of this book.

CONCLUSION

Baptism is at the heart of our life as a church. It is the sacrament that begins our life in Christ. It signifies all that Christ has done for us in his death, burial and resurrection. In the mystery of sacramental life in baptism, God joins us to Christ and his church. We are washed clean, given the life of the Spirit and clothed with Christ.

Baptism therefore demands our careful thought and prayer. It requires proper preparation, clear and creative enactment and fully committed follow-up, for the new life in Christ is to be lived out every second of every day for the remainder of our lives.

PREPARING TO RUN THIS COURSE

WHY RUN THIS COURSE?

Families bring babies and small children to church to be christened because it matters to them. They give a variety of reasons for this, some of the most common being:

- Wanting the child to be nurtured by godparents.

- Family tradition.

- Taking time to give thanks for their child and offer them to God for blessing and protection.

- Wanting the child to become part of the church and/or to begin a journey of faith.

Their deep desire is to give their child the best possible start in life and it is wonderful that they come to the church as a place that will help them. Here are some of the reasons families give for wanting to have a child christened:

'God knows that he's there and that we want him to be kept safe and looked after.'

'For him to have a religion and to be in the church because when I was younger, I used to go to ... Sunday school. I believe in God, and I'd like my son to believe in God as well even though my partner doesn't.'

'As soon as he was born really we were adamant we were going to have him christened ... It just felt natural that we have him done at the same church where we were married.'

'I knew I always wanted to have him christened ... I feel, for me, it's bringing him into the Church, but also to almost introduce him to God so that you know, God will look after him and keep him safe. So I do think it was really important. Definitely, to have him christened.'

'The first step of giving them a choice on faith and saying you know, you have been baptized into this faith. God knows you're out there and if you want him, he's there. If you don't, that's fine. It sounds silly, but for me it's a bit of protection. I feel like they've been blessed and someone is looking over them, you know, cause they've been introduced to God.'

Christening matters so much for these families that they make time to find their local church, get in touch, attend whatever preparation is offered, choose godparents, organize a party and bring their families and friends to church. They want the day, including the church service and the party, to be a special and memorable celebration of the birth and life of their unique and precious child.

Baptism, or christening, also matters to the church and to God, as we celebrate and welcome the arrival of a new member of our family. As with any special event in a family, it is a time to give thanks and show our love for each other. This day is the beginning of a new chapter in the life of faith of the family and the church as we all travel together as companions on the most exciting journey we could ever dream of.

If christening matters so much to families, to churches, and to God, it is worth spending time and effort making sure that everyone is as well prepared as possible. This will help to make sure that the christening day is special and memorable. Good preparation will also put in place some key foundations on which everyone can build as they work to keep the promises made in the service, loving and supporting each other in the months and years ahead, praying for each other, and giving the child everything they need to develop to spiritual maturity.

This course addresses three key topics to help families explore the full meaning of their child's christening, to make the day itself as special and memorable as possible and to suggest some simple ways in which their child's christening can shape them as a family. The topics are:

1. GETTING READY

   Exploring:

   • Why the family wants to have their child christened.

   • What they need to do to get ready.

   • The role of godparents and other important adults in the child's life.

2. THE BIG DAY

Exploring:

- The service itself.
- The meaning of some of the most significant features of the service.
- The promises that are being made.

3. THE JOURNEY CONTINUES

Exploring:

- The way children's needs change as they grow older.
- Sharing special times as a family.
- Church support and activities your church offers families.
- Sharing Bible stories with children.
- Praying with and for children.

In churches, or groups of churches, in which many children are baptized each year and where there are enough volunteers and other resources, the preparation could be run over three sessions, as outlined in this book. There are also options for organizing preparation in a single session for a group of families (see p. 141), and for one family on its own (see p. 163).

WHEN?

Each session should last approximately one and a half hours – about an hour of discussion and activities and 30 minutes for refreshments and informal conversation. This is an important time for building relationships and encouraging families to ask questions.

Some churches prefer to hold sessions in the evening (7.30–9 pm or 8–9.30 pm). Others find it easier to hold sessions on a Sunday afternoon, with teatime refreshments. If you choose this option, it's important to make sure any children have someone to take care of them and there are toys available.

The outlines begin with a time of discussion covering the core issues for each topic. After that, there is a set of extra materials to build on this discussion. You need to choose the activities that are most suitable for you, bearing in mind the facilities you have (e.g. there is always an option involving showing film clips) and the general preferences of parents in your area (do most of them enjoy discussions, or do they prefer something more practical and hands-on?).

IDEAL SIZE OF GROUP

A group session would ideally include six to twelve adults. This could include godparents if they are able to come. Attending the preparation sessions is a good opportunity for godparents to reflect on their role and to understand what it might mean to take it seriously.

WHO CAN LEAD IT?

The course can be led by any church member who has a gift for engaging with people and cares deeply about children and families. The minister or ministers who will be conducting the baptisms should be seen and introduced at some point, but they do not need to lead the sessions.

HOW MANY PEOPLE ARE REQUIRED TO RUN IT?

You will need a minimum of two people: one to lead the session and the other to serve refreshments, make sure that all the items for each session are in the right places when they are needed, and help out as required. If possible, it's good to have an additional person to make sure that everything runs smoothly and to chat informally with the families, listening to them and building relationships.

RECRUITING A TEAM

Time spent with families who rarely (if ever) come to church is an important 'shop window' for your church and for Christianity. It is essential to make sure that your team understands this and has the right skills. The person organizing refreshments and 'front of house' will need to be friendly and have a gift for relaxed hospitality. The leader of the sessions will need to be good at engaging with families and have skills in presenting ideas and information for groups to explore together. There are two ways to recruit the team:

1. Advertise in your church notices that you are looking for team members. This may bring forward suitable people you would never have thought of asking, but may also attract some whose skills would not be appropriate in this role. In the latter case, you need to be able to say no.

2. Approach people directly, knowing that they would do well in this role. The advantage of this option is that you only ask suitable people. However, there may be others you have not noticed who have gifts in this area.

CHOOSING A VENUE: CONSIDERATIONS

Your meeting space may be in the church itself or in a hall or meeting room, as long as there is room and chairs for people to sit comfortably in a circle.

It's important to:

- Clear away or hide any piles of furniture or junk.

- Make sure the temperature is comfortable: adjust the heating or open windows if necessary.

- Set out enough chairs for everyone to sit in a circle.

- If you are using any activities involving writing or drawing, you will need clipboards or tables for people to lean on, and paper, pens or pencils.

- If you are expecting children to come, put out suitable toys and books.

- Think about access to toilet facilities: if children are attending, you will need to consider the needs of small children, arrangements for nappy changing, etc.

INVITATIONS: WHO TO INVITE, HOW?

The sessions are for all parents of children being baptized. It can also be good to invite godparents, if they live locally enough. If there are older children in the family and the parents have already been through a preparation programme, it is still good to invite them, but you will need to decide how important it is for them to come this time. It may be more appropriate to use the material in this book for a single session with one family.

When parents contact the priest or the church office to ask for a christening, they are usually anxious to get a date in the diary. In my experience, they often see this as 'booking a venue' for their special day, and may be surprised that there is any need to meet anyone first, or to come to preparation sessions. It is very important to be clear in this first phone call or email exchange what the pattern is in your church. For example, the first email reply might say something along these lines:

Dear (name)

We are delighted to hear that you would like your child christened at (church name). This is such a special event that we like to make sure everyone has all the information they need.

As a first step (the priest or a member of your baptism preparation team) will be in touch to arrange a time to meet you. They will have a short chat with you about why christening matters to you and to the church and they will explain all the options and possible dates.

After that meeting, we will invite you to our next 'We Welcome You session(s) on the following date(s):

With love and prayers at this special time.

FOLLOW-UP AFTER THE COURSE

The research shows that many families are happy for the church to keep in touch after the christening. There are many ways to do this. Here are a few ideas:

- Members of your preparation team could visit each family a few weeks after the service to ask them how it went from their point of view, to remind them that you are praying for them and to make sure they have information about suitable activities and events.

- Send the child a birthday card and/or a card on the anniversary of the christening.

- Send invitations to activities and events. This could be done by letter, email, text or social media. When you meet the families, ask how they would prefer to be contacted.

- Invite the families to an annual celebration of the christening, including a short, noisy service and a tea party.

- Invite the families to come to church to mark the anniversary of the christening by lighting their child's candle in a service. For example, if you have a monthly all-age or family service, the lighting of candles could be a regular feature.

- Invite families and godparents to a special 'Godparents Sunday Service'.

SESSION 1: GETTING READY

———

AIM OF THE SESSION

The first session of this three-week programme is really important. It may be the first opportunity parents have to discover more about what having their child baptized means, not just on the day itself but in the years ahead. They will already have some ideas, thoughts and feelings, even if they can't express them well – or in the language the church uses. This session is a chance for them to ask questions and share their thoughts.

In this first session, the family will think about:

- Why they want to have their child christened.

- What they need to do to get ready.

- The role of godparents and other important adults in the child's life.

WHAT DOES CHRISTENING MEAN TODAY?

In the 1950s, about two out of every three babies in England were baptized, usually within a few weeks of birth. Today, far fewer families bring children to be baptized simply because it is the done thing. However, around one in six families still make this positive choice, often going against the trend among their peers.

The age at which a child is christened has also changed. Church of England statistics indicate that a family will often wait until a child is a few months old, or even until they feel that their family is complete, before asking for a christening[2]. The research findings from the Church of England's Baptism Project[3] show that for these families there is something special and significant about a christening that they value greatly. They do not feel that it can be replaced by an event such as a secular naming ceremony or a family party on its own. There is a sense that something important would be missing.

When researchers asked families what it meant to have their child christened, many replies reflected a deep sense of thanks for the gift of children and a desire to offer this thanks to something holy and other: in other words, to God. Parents naturally want to give their children the best possible start in life, and those who ask for a christening understand (without necessarily using this sort of language) that baptism can be an important part of laying these solid foundations. Parents also want their children to establish a sound set of moral values on which to base life choices and decisions as they grow up — godparents are understood to be particularly significant as role models and as people who will support their godchildren in developing a moral framework. In fact, according to the research, making sure their child has godparents is the number one reason parents give for wanting their child christened.

This first session includes opportunities for families to discuss and explore the role their chosen godparents can play in the future. Listening to families talk about the reasons for choosing particular godparents often gives insights into what matters most to them. They may want to reinforce family bonds and connections by choosing aunts and uncles. Others may invite friends who have supported them over the years to become part of their extended family in the role of godparents. Recently, I baptized the second child in a family. For the

---

[2] The CofE statistics are available at www.churchofengland.org/about-us/facts-stats/research-statistics.aspx.

[3] See www.churchsupporthub.org/baptism for more information.

older child, the parents chose godparents from within the family, partly at the suggestion of the grandparents. However, the parents had been disappointed that these godparents hadn't done anything more than would have been expected of them as family members; in addition, two of them lived on the other side of the world and hadn't met the child since the christening day. For the second child, they decided it mattered more to have godparents who would be close by, and would take the trouble to get to know their godchild and take a more active part in bringing them up.

When considering godparents for our own children, my husband and I chose people who we knew would care deeply about them, take time to build a special relationship with them and would pray for them. Each of these relationships has developed differently as our children have grown up and each godparent has become a special person in our children's lives: by listening to them, for example, or providing practical help, taking them on shopping trips to London, even giving them rides in a sports car; and, most importantly to us, holding them in their prayers. Given the importance of godparents in our own family, it should not have been a surprise to read the research and learn that this was also true for many other people. There are some important questions for churches to ask about finding ways to recognize the importance of this role and to support those who agree to become godparents.

As well as exploring the role of godparents, this first session is an opportunity for families to discover that baptism is the beginning of a journey that will continue for the rest of the child's life. In some ways this is similar to a wedding being a special event that marks the beginning of a marriage. Families usually spend a lot of time planning the christening day to make sure that it is a very special event. These preparation sessions are a good opportunity to encourage families to think about longer-term hopes and dreams for their child(ren) and the part that their baptism (including the promises that are made, the people involved, and the prayers offered in the service and over the years ahead) can play in fulfilling these.

A NOTE ON TERMINOLOGY: 'CHRISTENING' OR 'BAPTISM'?

These days, most families will use the word christening rather than the word baptism — in fact, it is over ten times more commonly used in internet searches. They will be buying christening cards, gifts, robes and cakes, and the term is used to cover the whole event, including the party afterwards, as well as the service. When talking to families, it may help to explain that the words 'baptism' and 'christening' both refer to the same important event in the child's life. The family's child will be baptized during a christening service; finding this out may be the first small step on a journey of discipleship. It is similar to the idea that a couple are married during a wedding service. It is very important to introduce these ideas gently, without making families feel as if they have made some sort of mistake by using the word christening. They are often afraid of appearing ignorant in front of church people, and speaking to them in the words they would use themselves can help to build their confidence.

The families may have questions about the content of the service itself. This will be covered in much more detail in the next session, but do take time to answer any specifics that may be worrying them.

CHRISTENING MATTERS ...

... TO FAMILIES

A christening is an important event in the life of a family. Most families take the planning of this event very seriously and work hard to make sure that it is a special and memorable day. As part of this, they are pleased when churches help them to prepare for the service itself. They also appreciate suggestions that will help them keep the meaning of the christening alive in the family for the years ahead. One family I visited proudly showed me the older children's baptism candles, beautifully displayed on stands on a shelf, and explained that they lit them for every birthday and on christening anniversaries to remember their church birthday.

... TO CHURCHES

A child's baptism on their christening day is important in the life of a church, as we welcome a new member into the family. We can do many things to make baptisms special and memorable for everyone, including:

- Taking seriously the family's desire to do things properly, including offering high-quality preparation.

- Making sure the service itself is special and welcoming.

- Investing time and effort in building relationships with families.

- Maintaining contact with the family after the event.

... TO GOD

As we support families who are preparing for a christening, we remember that this event also matters to God. It is good to hold the family in the prayers of all those involved in the preparations before, during and after the service. We can also encourage the family to pray. The material here includes a short prayer that they could use. There are very helpful resources for families and godparents at **www.churchofenglandchristenings.org**.

At Jesus' baptism, God spoke from the heavens and identified Jesus as his beloved Son, in whom his promises were being fulfilled. In a less dramatic way, a similar thing happens at every baptism. The candidate is recognized and affirmed in their identity as a beloved child made in the image of God, for whom God desires life in all its fullness. The promises made by God throughout human history are recalled in the words over the baptismal water, and we respond with our own promises and commitments. Baptism is, of course, a sacrament in which God's love is made visible in the actions, the words and the lives of those who have gathered for this special occasion.

RUNNING SESSION 1: MAIN SESSION

The material in this session will take about an hour to run. If you are meeting for an hour and a half, you may like to spend longer chatting informally and building relationships over refreshments. This will help you to get to know people better; you may find that someone who initially appears 'loud' is actually trying to cover up their anxiety, or that a quieter person is reflective rather than painfully shy.

For a longer session, you may want to add some of the suggested additional activities (see p. 62). For this first session in particular, when you don't yet know whether the group will be chatty or quieter in discussions, it may be helpful to have a 'spare' activity ready in case you have extra time to fill.

When planning the session, it is very important to know your context. In your community, are people confident with words, enjoying rich, complicated language? Or are they more likely to engage with hands-on activities? I minister in a team of five churches, and as might be expected there are differences between the communities they serve. In some of the churches people are likely to be very articulate, confident in answering complicated questions, but often quite anxious about any creative activity – 'I'm no good at art' would be a common reaction to a suggestion that they do some cutting and sticking. One of the churches serves a community in which far fewer people are graduates. More families here will engage with real enjoyment in active, participative ways of learning. They are not as articulate, and may be reluctant to read aloud, but will express deep and beautiful ideas in activities that give them space to move and engage physically.

1. SETTING UP BEFORE THE SESSION

First impressions really do matter and it is important to get everything ready before course participants start to arrive. If you and your team are relaxed and confident as you welcome everyone, this will help others to relax too. Make your meeting space as tidy, comfortable and welcoming as possible (see p. 38 for more details).

- Prepare the refreshments.
  - o Provide a choice of tea, coffee, decaffeinated coffee and cold drinks.
  - o Home-made cakes and biscuits are always popular if you can arrange this.
  - o It is good hospitality to have gluten-free options available.
  - o Some families will appreciate the option of fruit for any children.
  - o If children are coming, make sure you have cups appropriate to their age range, e.g beakers with lids for toddlers.
  - o It is sensible to have some kitchen towels, baby wipes or cloths available in case of accidents or sticky fingers.
  - o Provide name badges for everyone, including yourself and your team.
  - o Colourful lanyards with plastic holders for name cards will make it easy to identify your team and are available at a reasonable price on the internet.
  - o Sticky labels will be fine for the families.
- Look through the 'You will need' list for each of your chosen activities and make sure you have everything.

CORE PROGRAMME OVERVIEW: SESSION 1

Arrival and Welcome	15 minutes
Introduction	5 minutes
Getting Ready	10–15 minutes
Christening call	5 minutes
Why are we here	5 –10 minutes
Godparents	10–15 minutes
Closing prayer activity	5–10 minutes
	60–70 minutes plus discussion time

2. AS PEOPLE ARRIVE (10 MINS)

Families are likely to be anxious when they arrive. Some or all of these questions may be running through their minds:

- What is going to happen?

- Will there be difficult questions?

- If they don't know the 'right' answers, will their child still be christened?

- Will they have anything in common with the other people coming, or will they feel out of place?

- Do they need to be extra polite in front of church people?

- If their child(ren) are coming, will they behave?

A warm welcome to each person will help families begin to relax. These suggestions may help:

- Make sure that your church team is easy to identify (e.g. with colourful lanyards and name badges).

- Ask one of your team to stand at the door to invite people in and make sure they know where to collect refreshments and where to sit.

- Serve refreshments as people arrive. It can be a real challenge for families with young children to arrive at a precise time. There will almost always be an early arrival and some late ones. Chatting over refreshments is a good way to begin to build relationships and allows people to arrive comfortably over a period of time.

- Introduce families to each other as they arrive. Some of them may already know one another.

When everyone has arrived, move around the group and invite people to come and sit down in the circle of chairs. Make sure they are all sitting comfortably and that any babies and children have the things they need to be as happy as possible.

3. WELCOME AND INTRODUCTIONS (5 MINS)

At the start of the session, it is important to make sure everyone has a chance to learn other people's names and find out a bit about each other. The first activity is a gentle icebreaker to help them to begin to chat about something safe and familiar.

You will need:

- Pictures or cards with words to represent activities families enjoy. Make sure the activities represented are relevant in your context and the sort of things families there actually do together.

- Some blank cards and pens so that families can add their own choice of activities.

First, introduce the people who are helping at the session – the leaders, those serving refreshments, and anyone else in the room.

Then welcome the families and tell them how delighted you are that they have chosen to have their children christened.

Next, introduce the icebreaker activity. Put the picture cards out on a table or the floor in the middle of the group. Ask each family to choose a card representing something they enjoy doing together. If they have an idea that isn't on a card, ask them to take a blank one and represent their own idea. Take a card yourself.

Explain that you are going to invite each family to introduce themselves by giving their names (including their child or children) and saying which card they have chosen and why. Start with yourself, so that everyone can see what will happen. It's good to explain at this point why you are leading the session (for example, because you are the vicar or because you are the organizer for all the baptism preparation in your area). Show everyone the card you chose and explain why you chose it. Then turn to the person sitting next to you in the circle and ask them to introduce themselves and explain their choice of card.

When everyone has spoken, say a few words about how glad you are to know a little about the people who are here and how much you are looking forward to getting to know them better over the next two sessions.

4. INTRODUCTION TO THE SESSION (5 MINS)

It is important for people to have a general overview of what is going to be covered and to be clear about any 'ground rules', including confidentiality.

Explain that this is the first of three sessions. In this first session, participants will have an opportunity to think about why they want to have their child christened, what they need to do to get ready, and the role of godparents and other important adults in the child's life. The second session will go through what will happen in church on the christening day. The final session will look at the months and years ahead as the child grows up.

Tell the group that you know it can be difficult to organize coming out three times, but you really appreciate that they have made the effort. Attending the course will help make their child's christening day as significant and memorable as it possibly can be.

Invite the families to ask any questions, and sat that they can ask questions at any point during the sessions. Also let them know who to contact if they have questions at any other time.

Make it clear that everything said in the sessions should be treated as confidential to the group and not gossiped about. Emphasize that while everyone should feel that they can be honest, this is not the right place to be pouring out heart and soul. People should only speak about things that they are happy for everyone in the group to know.

Explain that the words 'christening' and 'baptism' refer to the same special event in a child's life. Christening is a traditional word to describe the fact that the child will be welcomed as a member of the church. Baptism is the word used more often in churches. It means to be dipped or immersed and refers to the way water is used in the church service.

Check whether anyone has any questions and then tell the group that you are going to move on to the main part of the session, starting by remembering how they got ready for the arrival of the new baby or a new member of the family. (Note: It is important to be sensitive about the different situations of families in the group. For example, a family may have adopted a child, or there may be a new partner who was not part of the family at the time of the birth.)

5. GETTING READY FOR THE NEW ARRIVAL
(10-15 MINS, DEPENDING ON THE SIZE OF THE GROUP)

You will need:

- Flipchart and pens, or computer and projector.
- Small cards, pens and 'lucky dip' bag (e.g. a school PE kit bag).

Invite people to give their answers to the following questions. If there are more than two or three families, it might be helpful to note the answers on a flipchart or screen.

- How did you get ready for the arrival of the child who is to be christened? Encourage suggestions out loud or ask everyone to write one idea on a small card and put them all in a 'lucky dip' bag. Invite each person in turn to take out a card and say whether they did this thing and why (or why not). If people look a bit blank, you could offer some suggestions to get started, e.g. buying a cot, decorating a room, learning how to change a nappy, going to ante-natal classes, choosing a name.

- How did you choose the child's name? Go round the group one family at a time.

6. CHRISTENING CALL (5 MINS)

You will need:

- Instruments or phone sounds to indicate right and wrong answers (or use your own voice), similar to those used on TV shows, e.g. 'Wac wac oops' or a hooter for a wrong answer, a ping or a bell for a right one. If you type 'free sound effects download' into a search engine, you will find a good choice online and you may be able to use these on your mobile phone. Hooters are often available in party shops and office supply shops and websites often stock bells for reception desks.

- Christening checklist (see opposite; also available as photocopiable sheet 1.1, p. 70.

CHRISTENING CHECKLIST

Choose godparents

Contact the church

Book a hall for the party

Invite friends and family

Go to preparation sessions

Sort out clothes for everyone

Ask someone to take photos

Order a cake

Go to church before the big day

Explain that this activity is based on the TV game show *Family Fortunes*. The families need to try to guess the most common things that people do when they are getting ready for a christening. You could split the group into two teams for fun.

Ask the first team to suggest something that might be on the list.

Say something like, 'We asked a hundred families, what did you do to get ready for your child's christening? You said (*repeat the first family's answer*). Our survey says (*hooter for answer not on your list, bell for one that is on your list*).'

Move on to the other team.

When each team has had three goes, read out the missing answers. Ask whether they can think of anything else that should have been on the list. Say that a christening day is a very special occasion, and getting ready can be a busy time, but it is good to remember that it is about starting a lifetime journey of finding out more about following Jesus.

7. WHY ARE WE HERE? (5–10 MINS)

You will need:

Either (*in groups that might prefer quieter activities, with more personal reflection – or if space is very limited*) enough copies for one for each adult of the sheet of reasons for having a child christened (see below or photocopiable sheet 1.2 for list, p. 71), pens.

Or (*in groups that like to engage in a more active, practical way*) a large copy of the sheet of reasons, and coloured pens or stickers.

Either: Make a copy of the checklist on page 71 and ask each person to tick their reasons before you discuss their answers.

Or: Make a large copy on a flipchart sheet or a piece of lining paper and ask people to put a tick or a sticky star or dot next to the reasons they would give. When they have finished, look at which reasons have the most ticks (or stickers) and encourage people to say why they chose them.

HOW MUCH DID EACH OF THE FOLLOWING INFLUENCE YOUR DECISION TO HAVE YOUR CHILD BAPTIZED AT A CHRISTENING?
(A lot, a little, not at all)

- Family tradition
- Encouragement from family
- Thanksgiving for the birth of your child
- Wanting godparents for your child
- Wanting your child to belong in the church
- To help protect your child in life
- Wanting a good start for your child

- To make sure your child has a place in heaven

- To have a party, celebrating with family and friends

- To mark the start of a journey of faith for your child

- To have a blessing for your child

- To help your child choose to be a Christian in future

- To do the same thing as my friends are doing

- To support what my partner wants to happen

Highlight the fact that many families think it is important for their children to have godparents and this is one of the reasons they give for wanting a christening. Godparents are a very significant part of the baptism service and can have a valuable role in their godchildren's lives over the years ahead. This leads us to the next section.

8. GODPARENTS (10–15 MINS)

Godparents are very important. Parents often think very carefully before choosing people they trust to take a special interest in their child, act as good role models and play an important part in the life of the family. Churches also take the role of godparents very seriously, which is why there are some rules and guidelines about who can be a godparent when a child is baptized. You can find advice about this at **www.churchofenglandchristenings.org/ for-parents/choosing-godparents**.

It is good practice for churches to make the requirements clear at a very early stage of the enquiry, so that families are aware of them before this preparation session. This is a good opportunity to check whether the families have any questions. In particular, it may be worth checking that the people they have in mind do meet these requirements. If necessary, you may need to discuss this at a separate time with any families whose situation is complicated.

It is also worth making sure that people understand the difference between godparents and legal guardians. There is widespread confusion about the role of godparents if anything should happen to the child's parents. Being a godparent is not the same as being a legal guardian. It may be helpful to point out that if families choose as godparents people they would like to take care of their children should the need arise, they should also appoint them as legal guardians in their wills.

It would then be good to spend some time discussing the following questions:

- Who have you chosen as godparents?

- Why have you chosen these people?

- What are you hoping they will do over the years?

If your group would be happier exploring this in a more active way, use the following simple suggestion:

You will need:

- Plastic building bricks (e.g. Duplo, MegaBlocks or similar).

- Whiteboard marker pens.

Good godparents can help build solid foundations for a child's life. Ask people to think about the qualities they are looking for in their children's godparents. Use the marker pens to write each quality on a brick and invite the families to build these bricks together to make the foundations of a house. Examples of qualities families are looking for might include:

- A good role model.

- Someone to talk to outside the family.

- Someone who buys good presents.

- Someone who would pray for their godchild.

- Someone who would take the child to church.

'We wanted both of our children to have godparents when they were christened. It was important to us to have other key people in their lives that could guide, support and influence them. A godparent is someone who is actively involved in a child's life and is there for them. To us choosing a godparent was someone who would be there for our children, who are responsible, sensible and supportive individuals who would want the best for them'.

9. CLOSING PRAYER (5–10 MINS)

Give a brief summary of everything you have covered, including why participants want to have their child christened, what they need to do to get ready and the role of godparents.

Thank everyone for all their ideas and contributions to the conversation.

Explain that to close the session you are going to gather together everything you have discussed, and the preparations still to come, and bring them all to God in prayer. This might be the very first time some people in the group have consciously offered any sort of prayer, so it is important to make sure that they feel safe and comfortable. Reassure them that prayer doesn't have to be complicated; it can be as simple as a tiny thought that you send to God. Explain that it is sometimes helpful to use symbols or actions to help to focus our minds and hearts on what really matters to us and to God.

PRAYING WITH THE BIG SYMBOLS OF BAPTISM

The baptism service uses three big symbols: oil, water and light. You could use one at each preparation session, or use the same activity at each session, referring to all three in one prayer.

Oil for preparation, protection and holiness

Oil is used in many baptism services as a symbol of preparation and protection, drawing attention to all that is special, unique and holy about the child.

You could invite the parents to use oil to make the sign of the cross on the back of each other's hands as a symbol of their own preparation for the christening day.

A PRAYER ACTIVITY USING OIL, WATER AND LIGHT

You will need:

- An empty jam jar with lid (a short, fat jar is less likely to get knocked over than a tall, thin one).

- Pens that will write on glass (most permanent markers are fine).

- Enough olive oil to half fill the jar.

- A 100 per cent cotton wick — you can buy wicks in craft shops, or you could make your own from a strip of fabric or a piece of an old cotton sock. It's important to use 100 per cent cotton, though — other materials might give off nasty fumes when burned.

- Water.

- A sharp knife or compass and a pair of scissors.

Before the session: Make a hole in the jam-jar lid, using a skewer, drill or gimlet. The hole needs to be just big enough to pull the wick through but not so big that it falls back through it. Pull the wick through so that about half an inch is sticking out and the rest is dangling below.

Instructions for making a prayer lamp:

- Invite the families to write the names of the children being baptized on the jar.

- Half fill the jar with water. Tell the families that water is very important in the baptism service. It reminds us of being cleaned and refreshed and starting something new.

- Top up with olive oil and leave to settle into two layers, with the oil floating on top of the water. Say that oil is also important in the baptism service. It is used to make the sign of the cross on the child as a symbol of being prepared and protected. It is also a way of focusing everyone's attention on everything that is special and holy about the child.

- Measure the distance from the lid down to the water level and cut the dangling bit of wick a little bit shorter. It should reach almost to the bottom of the oil, but not into the water.

- Screw on the lid with wick attached.

- Wait a while for the oil to soak fully into the wick. You could read the prayer below while you are waiting.

- Light the lamp. Explain that light is the final big symbol in the baptism service. The child will be given a lit candle to take out into the world to remind them that they carry the light of Christ with them for the rest of their lives.

- Explain that you are going to say a short prayer. Everyone is invited to repeat 'Amen' after you at the end, as a way of saying that this is their prayer too. Say the following words, or something similar:

Loving God, we thank you for (say all the children's names).

We pray for them as we prepare for their christenings.

Help us to pay attention to everything that is special and holy about them,

to get ready for the new journey that starts on the christening day

and to take the light of Christ with us for the rest of our lives.

Amen.

AN ALTERNATIVE PRAYER ACTIVITY USING OIL, WATER AND LIGHT

You will need:

- A cloth.

- A bottle of olive oil or a church oil stock.

- A bowl (ideally a clear one).

- A bottle of water.

- A candle and matches or a lighter (make sure it is in a suitable candle holder or on a heatproof mat).

Spread out the cloth, saying:

As we spread out this cloth, we bring to God all our hopes and dreams, all our fears and worries.

Put the container of oil on the cloth, saying:

As we bring oil for healing and holiness, we ask God to bless our children, our families, and our homes.

Put the bowl on the cloth, pour in the water, saying:

As we bring water for refreshment and cleansing, we ask God to fill us with his love and his life.

Put the candle on the cloth and light it, saying:

As we bring light to show us the way, we ask God to show us how to help our children to live well.

Spend a few moments in quiet, looking at the items. Draw the time of prayer to a close by saying:

Loving God,

We pray for your love and peace for everyone here

as we leave this place and as we live our lives, until we meet again.

We pray in the name of your Son, Jesus. **Amen.**

PRAYER CARD

Read a prayer together. You could light a candle before you begin.

Suggested prayers:

Loving God,

we pray for your blessing on our family

as we prepare for the christening of our child.

Help us to follow Jesus together.

Amen.

Or this one from the website **www.churchofenglandchristenings.org/prayers**

Creator God,

We thank you for the gift of the life of this child who is to be baptized.

May your blessing of peace and joy be with them

and protect them all of their days.

We make this prayer in the name of your Son, Jesus.

Amen.

You could give each family a prayer card (see photocopiable sheet 1.3, p. 72).
Encourage them to put it somewhere they will see it every day (if you attach
a magnet, they could easily stick it to their fridge) and read it, perhaps at
mealtimes or bedtime.

SESSION 1: ADDITIONAL MATERIAL

The material in the main session is designed to last for about an hour. However, this will vary depending on the size of group and how much they talk. If you are expecting only a couple of families, it would be sensible to have one or two extra activities ready. In a larger group, or with chatty group members, you may have to work hard to ensure that the discussions come to a close in time to do something that will engage people in a different way.

These additional materials are to use if you will have time to fill; or they could replace sections of the main material. For example, some groups may prefer to watch and discuss a film clip rather than doing the icebreaker activity. You could also use them to create additional sessions.

1. FIRST STEPS ON A JOURNEY (10 MINS)

You will need:

- The shoes people are already wearing (no need to bring anything).
- You could also have pictures of different shoes (e.g. for running, hiking, ice skating, parties, the beach, etc.).

The christening is not just a single very special day. It is the beginning of a journey that will last for the rest of a child's life.

Talk with the group about the kinds of shoes required for different journeys. Perhaps look at the pictures you have brought and discuss the activities to which they are suited. Invite the group to look at each other's shoes. Ask what these shoes tell us about each person's journey to get here. For example, if someone is wearing sensible outdoor shoes or trainers, they might have walked to the venue. Someone in high heels is perhaps less likely to have walked very far.

Ask the families what sort of shoes they buy for their children. Have they already started buying them different types of shoes for different occasions or activities?

For example, a toddler might have wellies or beach shoes. Even a small baby might have a pair of party shoes.

Explain that the whole of the child's life will be a journey. They will need different support and equipment at various points of their life. Bringing a child to be christened is one way of giving them some of the equipment they will use on their journey through life. It is a little bit like making sure you have the right shoes ready for each stage of your journey.

Ask the families to suggest different things that might happen in their children's lives that would need special support and equipment. What sort of shoes might suit these stages best – for example, there are times in our lives for party shoes and other times when we need sturdy hiking boots.

If you have brought a collection of pictures of shoes, you could ask families to pick one and talk about how these shoes would help their child.

Ask the families in what way are they hoping that the christening service will give their child a good start on their journey through life.

Give a brief summary of the answers families have given, pointing out the ideas they had in common and any differences. Say that all families and all children are different in their own special ways, but one thing that the families are likely to have in common is that they want the best for their children. Having children christened can be an important part of that. (This could be a good introduction to the section headed 'Christening call' or 'Why are we here?').

2. FILM CLIP (10 MINS)

If you have the equipment to play film clips, show one that includes people getting ready for an adventure. A baptism is not only a special event; it is the beginning of a great adventure.

It is important to choose a clip that is right for your context and your group. When we asked a dad to read through this material, he was keen to avoid the film equivalents of tea lights and wafty fabrics, and suggested that any of the scenes in which James Bond receives new equipment from Q (the Quartermaster) would work well. (The films up to and including *The Living Daylights* (1987) were all rated PG. The relevant scene in *Goldfinger* begins at 22 mins 14 secs and ends at 24 mins 37 secs.)

After watching the clip, discuss the equipment people took and how useful it turned out to be. What might you have taken to prepare for this adventure?

Alternatively, you could watch the section from the start of Wallace and Gromit's *A Grand Day Out* just before they launch the rocket. Wallace and Gromit have built a rocket to visit the moon for fresh supplies of cheese, but they almost forget the crackers. What would you have to go back for to be properly prepared for an adventure?

3. IMPORTANT PEOPLE IN MY LIFE (20 MINS)

You will need:

- 'My Life' sheet (one for each adult) (see photocopiable sheet 1.4, p. 73).

- Pens or pencils.

At their baptism, a child is surrounded by people who promise to take care of them. The godparents take on a very special role and families hope that they will play a significant part in the child's life as they grow up.

Give each person a copy of the sheet headed 'My Life'. Ask them to think about the most important events in their lives, noting three to five for each period. Then ask them to think about important people in their lives – who were the key influences for each period?

Ask them all to look at a 'My Life' sheet that has not been filled in. Invite them to think quietly for a few minutes about what important things they hope their child might write about when they have grown up. After a time of silence, invite them to think about the people they hope their child might name as important influences.

Invite the group to share any thoughts they would like the others to hear. Remember that some people may have found their memories painful. It would be good to remind everyone that whatever anyone shares must be kept confidential to this group.

4. FOOTPRINTS PICTURE (10 MINS)

You will need:

- Sheets of coloured A4 paper (several for each family).

- Sheets of A3 card or paper (one for each family).

- Pencils or pens.

- Scissors.

- Glue.

- Coloured pens or markers.

Baptism is the start of a journey into the future, and everyone who was at the christening walks along together.

Give each family a selection of sheets of coloured A4 paper. Invite the adults to draw round their own feet (left and right) on the coloured paper and cut out the shapes.

Give each family a sheet of A3 paper or card and ask them to stick the footprints onto it so that they form a ring round an empty space in the centre.

Invite them to draw round their child's feet, either now or when they get home and stick these footprints into the centre of the picture.

Write the following words on the picture, writing over all the footprints:

N (child's name)

We love you and we walk with you.

5. BIBLE REFLECTION: THE JOURNEY INTO PARENTHOOD (20 MINS)

The parable of the lost son (Luke 15.11–32) covers some of the most challenging aspects of family life and invites us to understand these in relationship to God's love for his children. In a baptism preparation group, it could be the first time some people have heard it. I have worked with baptism families who found this story hugely helpful, opening up some very important issues. In a couple of cases, we continued to work through these issues in conversations over several weeks or months, and I have clear memories of their insights and questions several years later. These were not churchgoing families, and only a few of them knew the story already, but it touched them deeply.

Invite each person to name something that has changed in their lives because they are now a parent. Encourage people to enjoy sharing stories of the joys and challenges they face.

Ask how they felt the first time they held their new child. Parenting is a complicated mixture of joy and pain, love and fear, mystery and danger, and many other things. One story in the Bible captures many aspects of this.

Read Luke 15.11–32 (the parable of the lost son) in a modern translation or paraphrase, such as *The New Living Translation* or *The Message*. You might prefer to use a children's version, such as *The Lion Storyteller Bible*.[4] There is also a creative retelling of the story in *Festivals Together* by Sandra Millar.[5]

Invite everyone to sit in silence for a few minutes. Discuss some or all of the following questions:

- How might the father have felt when his younger son left home?

- How might the younger son have been feeling when he came home?

- What did he expect to happen when he returned?

---

[4] Bob Hartman, *The Lion Storyteller Bible*, Lion, 2013.

[5] Sandra Millar, *Festivals Together*, SPCK, 2012.

- How might the father have felt when he saw his son coming?

- Where is the mother in this story?

- Why did the older brother react the way he did?

- Who do you relate to most closely in this story?

- Do you know anyone who would behave as the father did?

- What can we learn about parenthood from this story?

6. A MEMORY BOOK (5 MINS)

You will need:

- Scrapbook pages or photo albums.

- Paper (a wide variety of colours and backgrounds is available in many craft shops or on the internet).

- Scissors.

- Pens.

- Glue.

An album of photos or a scrapbook telling the story of the christening day is a gift that will be treasured by the family. It will also be a record for the child to which they can return as as they grow up. Many of the children who come to be christened are old enough to share this as a bedtime story, which will help to keep alive their own memories of the event. When families have made books like this, children have sometimes taken them into school years later when the class has been learning about babies.

You could give out these books to the families for them to make at home, or you could start them together as an additional activity. You could add to them in the next two preparation sessions.

Give each family a photo album or a set of scrapbook pages. If you know anyone, perhaps a member of the congregation, who makes scrapbooks as a hobby, it might be good to involve them. Perhaps they could come to the session and show the families some examples of their work and share some simple ideas and tips to give the families extra confidence and inspiration.

If you are planning to use this activity, ask families in advance to bring photos with them. When I have used this activity, families have brought all sorts of lovely things to include, such as identity bracelets from hospital, drawings of the new baby by older brothers and sisters, and a card made by someone very special to the family who could not come to the baptism.

AND FINALLY …

By the end of this first session, you will have begun to get to know the families and how they are going to work together. This should make it easier to choose activities to suit your group for the next two sessions.

You will also have covered some important ground, such as, in particular, understanding why these families have chosen to have their child baptized, helping them to make sure everything is ready for the christening day, and exploring the role of godparents.

PHOTOCOPIABLE MATERIAL
FOR SESSION 1

CHRISTENING CHECKLIST

Choose godparents ☐

Contact the church ☐

Book a hall for the party ☐

Invite friends and family ☐

Go to preparation sessions ☐

Sort out clothes for everyone ☐

Ask someone to take photos ☐

Order a cake ☐

Go to church before the big day ☐

HOW MUCH DID EACH OF THE FOLLOWING INFLUENCE YOUR DECISION TO HAVE YOUR CHILD BAPTIZED AT A CHRISTENING?

	A lot	A little	Not at all
Family tradition			
Encouragement from family			
Thanksgiving for the birth of your child			
Wanting godparents for your child			
Wanting your child to belong in the church			
To help protect your child in life			
Wanting a good start for your child			
To make sure your child has a place in heaven			
To have a party, celebrating with family and friends			
To mark the start of a journey of faith for your child			
To have a blessing for your child			
To help your child choose to be a Christian in future			
To do the same thing as my friends are doing			
To support what my partner wants to happen			

Loving God,

we pray for your blessing on our family

as we prepare for the christening of our child.

Help us to follow Jesus together.

Amen.

Creator God,

We thank you for the gift of the life of this child

who is to be baptized.

May your blessing of peace and joy be with them

and protect them all of their days.

We make this prayer in the name of your Son, Jesus.

Amen.

PHOTOCOPIABLE SHEET 1.4
'MY LIFE'
(to use with 'Important people in my life', p. 64)

MY LIFE

BIRTH

MAJOR EVENTS (3-5 in each time period)	IMPORTANT PEOPLE

0-10 years

....

....

....

....

....

10-20 years

....

....

....

....

....

20 years - now

....

....

....

....

....

PRESENT DAY

SESSION 2: THE BIG DAY

A christening day is a very significant event in a family's life. They will remember it for a long time, treasuring photos and special gifts. Church-based conversations and literature often focus on the words used in the baptism service, both in the liturgy and in the talk or sermon. In conversations with clergy colleagues and people involved in organizing baptisms, I often hear questions such as: 'Will the families understand what they are saying?' 'Do they mean the promises they make?' 'How can we use the sermon to teach them the things that really matter?' However, there is far more to baptism than the words that are used. There is huge depth and meaning to each of the symbols and a full human response to all of this is far more than an intellectual understanding of the language.

The whole environment adds to the family's impressions and memories. For example, the way in which they are (or are not) made to feel welcome and the comfort (or not) of the building are very important. I spoke recently to a family preparing to have their second child baptized who said that they would like the service to be 'as lovely as the last one'. When I asked what they remembered, they said, 'Everyone was so friendly and it made it all feel very special. Nobody made us feel stupid for not knowing what to do, so we really relaxed and loved everything about it. We still light our candle on important days.' Their memories were not of the words that had been spoken or the promises made, but they were still significant and related to some of the central themes of baptism – being welcomed as a new member of the community, paying attention to what is holy and special about the child, and taking the light of Christ to shine for the rest of the child's life.

Families say that they like the service to include formal language because they want the christening to be done 'properly'. After a very informal baptism service held in one of my churches, where our intention had been to make a family with no experience of church feel relaxed, the parents expressed some disappointment. They said they had wanted to feel that they had come into the 'front room of granny's house', which was for special occasions; instead it had felt more like being in the playroom. This was a very helpful reminder that churches and families may have different ideas about what families really need and want.

It is important to strike the right balance between honouring the family's wish to do things properly while also being warm and welcoming, and making sure that the family feels as engaged and involved as possible. At a recent baptism, two older sisters helped me for the whole service. As we moved around the building, I explained quietly what help I would need next ('I need you to hold a special silver pot. It's got some oil in it and we're going to use some to draw a cross on your sister's forehead to show how special she is,' etc.). The sound desk person accidentally left my microphone on, so the whole church heard this running conversation. Afterwards, someone in the christening party told me that they would always remember the way the girls had helped, and that my conversations with them had helped them understand what mattered at each point of the service.

For the families, the most important part of baptism preparation is to find out what will happen in the service. They often feel anxious about not knowing what to do or worrying how their children will behave. Knowing what is going to happen helps them to be more confident. As long as they have been given basic information about the running order and they know when they need to stand up and so on, families usually say that they are completely satisfied that they have had enough preparation.

THE AIM OF THE SESSION

This second session includes an overview of the service itself, adding more information about what is happening to help make the day as meaningful and memorable as possible.

During this second session, the family will:

- Find out more about what will happen in the service.

  o They will think about things they remember from any other church services they have been to and play a simple game to reflect on how they want their child's christening to be remembered.

  o You will give a brief run-through of your local baptism service.

- Explore more fully the meaning of some of the most significant features of the service.

  o There is a choice of two activities to engage the families in this, either packing a bag to prepare for a journey or thinking about the gifts a child is given in baptism.

- Use a simple activity to reflect on the promises that are being made.

THE SERVICE MATTERS ...

... TO FAMILIES

Families want to bring their children to be christened at a baptism service that welcomes them and their child into church and feels like a special occasion.

> 'It was nice that it was part of the morning service because then it was like my son was welcomed into the church and everyone saw him. I think it wasn't just like you go in, you have your little ceremony in the church, and go out again. It was part of the everyday life of the church as it should be.'

… TO CHURCHES

Welcoming a new member into our church family is one of the most important things we can do. Many families speak about the christening as an important step on their child's journey of faith and it is good to reflect this in the service. In general, families prefer the service to be traditional, saying that they consider this to be more proper and meaningful than a modern service could be.

Whatever the style, it is important for churches to do all they can to make services relaxed and friendly without losing the sense of the significance of the occasion and without speaking down to the family.

> 'Traditional is more meaningful. Nowadays everything seems too dumbed down or made to be in such a way that it doesn't offend anyone.'

The baptism service includes some of the central symbols, actions and words of our faith. The whole congregation, many of whom will have been baptized themselves, is invited to remember our own identity as beloved children of God.

… TO GOD

God speaks us into being and calls us to be his children. As we hear and receive God's invitation, the most appropriate human response is worship. In worship, we pay attention to our encounter with God and are transformed in the experience. All worship and church services matter to God. In a baptism service, God is with us as we welcome a new member into his family.

RUNNING SESSION 2: MAIN SESSION

The material in this session will take about an hour to run. If you are meeting for an hour and a half, you may like to spend longer over refreshments. However, walking through the service is very important, and families may have more questions than in other sessions. It would be good to make sure you have plenty of time to listen carefully to their concerns and to respond to them appropriately. There are some suggested additional activities that can be used if these would work better for your group or if you have extra time.

It could be helpful to hold some or all of this session in your church building. It would give the families an opportunity to walk through the service in the place where it will happen. However, you need to think about the following:

- Is the church space warm enough for people to sit in it for more than an hour without their coats on?

- Is there a space in which people can sit in a circle for a discussion?

- Can you serve refreshments there?

- If children are coming, is this a safe space for them? Is there a place for them to play safely?

- Are all the families having their children baptized in the same building? If your church is part of a wider group or team, baptisms may take place in several buildings. In this case, would it work to use just one of them, or would it be better to hold the session in another hall or room?

- You could use the church for only part of the session.

  Either of the following outlines could work:

  o Meet in church to walk through the baptism service. Move to another hall or room for refreshments and the rest of the session.

  o Meet in another hall or room for refreshments and all of Session 2 apart from the overview of the service, and then move to the church to walk through the service.

1. SETTING UP BEFORE THE SESSION

It is important to make sure that you take as much care over this as you did for the first session, and address any problems that came up. For example, if the way you set out your chairs meant that someone could not see well, avoid this by moving the chairs into a better position. You may also have a clearer idea of what toys and books would be most appropriate for any children who are likely to attend.

If you are holding some or all of this session in church, it is important to go through the same checklist for setting up, making sure that the space is as tidy, comfortable and welcoming as possible, that refreshments and activities are ready and waiting, and that you and your team are visible and ready to welcome everyone.

CORE PROGRAMME OVERVIEW: SESSION 2

Arrival and Welcome	15 minutes
Introduction	5 minutes
Experience and expectations	10 minutes

What will happen in the service:
    Packing for a journey OR
    Christening gifts
	10–15 minutes

Promises, promises	10 minutes
What happens when	10 minutes
Closing prayer activity	5–10 minutes
	70 minutes plus discussion time

2. AS PEOPLE ARRIVE (10 MINS)

If everything has gone well at the first session, families will be more relaxed for this one. However, there may be some new people who could not come last time and it is important to ensure that they are welcomed and feel that they can become part of the group.

3. WELCOME AND INTRODUCTIONS (5 MINS)

You will need:

- A list of what was covered in Session 1 (see photocopiable sheet 2.1, p. 99).
- Marker pens or sticky coloured dots or stars.

Introduce all the people who are helping at the session – the leaders, those serving refreshments, and anyone else in the room. It would be good to wear name badges. You may have introduced yourselves last week, but some people may not have been there and not everyone will remember.

Welcome the families and tell them how much you enjoyed last week, how good it is to see them again (and to meet anyone who is new to the group), and how much you are looking forward to this session.

Display a large copy of the list of topics covered in Session 1.

Ask everyone to tick with a pen or add a coloured dot or star next to the thing that sticks most in their minds from the last session.

Invite each person to find someone from another family (swapping seats if necessary) and talk to them about which item on the list they ticked and why.

4. INTRODUCTION TO THE SESSION (5 MINS)

Explain that this is the second of three sessions. Last time, we talked about getting ready for the christening day and the special role of godparents. In this session, we will go through what happens in the service itself and what it means. Next time, we will begin to get ready for the months and years ahead. Say that you hope that this will make the service even more special and significant.

Remind everyone that everything said in the sessions should be treated as confidential to the group and not gossiped about. While everyone should feel able to be honest, this is not the right place to be pouring out heart and soul. Explain that people should only speak about things that they are happy for everyone in the group to know. (It is particularly important to spell this out again if there is anyone new to the group.)

5. EXPERIENCE AND EXPECTATIONS (10 MINS)

You will need:

- A dice.
- A copy of the list of instructions for each roll of the dice (see below; also available as photocopiable sheet 2.2, p. 100).

EXPERIENCE AND EXPECTATIONS GAME
Instructions for rolling the dice

If you roll a ...	Name one thing that ...
1	... you like about church.
2	... you think churches could do better.
3	... you remember about the first time you went to church.
4	... you remember about the last time you visited a church.
5	... you are hoping for at your child's christening.
6	... you are worried about for your child's christening.

Members of the group will have had a variety of experiences of coming to church for other services, ranging from none at all, to those who have attended weddings, funerals and other family events, those who come at Christmas and other special services, and regular members of the congregation. This simple activity will draw on those experiences to help families think about their hopes and anxieties for their child's baptism in a christening service.

Invite each member of the group in turn to roll the dice and answer the question that goes with that number. If anyone can't think of an answer, ask them whether there is a question they would rather have. If not, that's fine; simply move on without making any fuss.

Ask what people are hoping their guests will remember most about their family's service.

6. WHAT WILL HAPPEN IN THE SERVICE?

Families are often anxious that they might not 'get things right'. As long as someone has run through the service with them, they are likely to be satisfied with even a small amount of baptism preparation. We strongly recommend that you use one of the two activities below – 'Packing for a journey' or 'Christening gifts' (p. 88) – making sure that it matches accurately the way in which baptism services are conducted in your church. Follow this with 'Promises, promises' (p. 90).

PACKING FOR A JOURNEY (10–15 MINS)

You will need:
- A child's bag.
- Flipchart or screen.
- The following items: map and/or guidebook; Bible; photograph of a group of friends; sun cream; the oil that will be used in the service; bottle of water; torch; a candle like the ones you give to baptism families. If the session is in church, you could put each item in the appropriate place (see note in brackets), and walk from place to place to talk about each item and put it in the bag.

For each item there is a short additional activity that can be used if you have time available or if your group enjoys activity more than word-based explanations.

Ask the families to imagine that they are going on a long journey. What would they need to pack to take with them? Write up a list of suggestions on a flipchart or screen.

Explain that the service in which their children will be baptized is a way of packing some of the things their child will need on their journey through life.

- **Map, guidebook and Bible** (the place where people stand to read from the Bible, e.g. a lectern): The first item that will be 'packed' during the service is a map or guidebook. We need directions to help us find the right path, and guidebooks give us interesting information about the places we visit. The Bible is a map and a guidebook to help us live a Christian way of life. We will hear a reading from it near the start of the service. *Invite someone to put the map, guidebook and Bible in the bag.*

Additional activity: Treasure map

You will need:

- Treasure map (see photocopiable sheet 2.3, p. 101).
- Small piece of paper for each person (they need to fit inside the grid squares).
- Pens or pencils.
- Dice.
- A small prize.

  o Give each person a small piece of paper and ask them to write their name on it.

  o Invite them to choose a square on the treasure map and place their name paper on it.

  o Roll the dice to find out which row of the map the treasure is hidden on.

  o Roll the dice again to find out which column of the map the treasure is hidden on.

o If someone has chosen that square, they have found the treasure and win the small prize.

o If nobody has chosen that square, the winner is the person who has chosen the nearest one.

- **Photograph of a group of friends** (the place where the presentation of candidates takes place, e.g. the chancel step or by the font): When we go on a long journey, it's good to travel with friends – people to share the experience with and remember it afterwards, to have fun with and to help us if we get into trouble. At the christening service in which your children will be baptized, there will be three groups of people who will be your children's travelling companions from that day on:

o **The godparents**, who will make a public commitment to support the children as they grow up and to help them live a Christian life.

o **Other family and friends**, who will have gathered together to share this special day and will continue to care about you and your children.

o **The church congregation** (or their representatives if the baptism takes place outside the main service), who will welcome your children as new members of our community. They will also make a commitment to support your children and their parents and godparents. *Invite someone to put the photo in the bag.*

Additional activity: 'I love my child with a ...'

This simple activity reminds us of the huge number of reasons why we love our children and the things that help to bind us together through the journey of life.

o Choose a letter of the alphabet.

o Start the sentence 'I love my child with a (*chosen letter*) because he/she is (*choose a word that begins with that letter*)',

> e.g. 'I love my child with an L because he is lovely.'
>
> o Ask the next person round to say the same sentence, but use a different word, e.g. 'I love my child with an L because she is always laughing.'
>
> o When it starts getting difficult to come up with new words, choose a different letter.

- **Sun cream and oil** (the place where candidates are anointed, e.g. the chancel step or by the font): If our journey takes our family to sunny places, we make sure our children are covered in sun cream to protect their skin. In the service, the children will be marked with oil as a symbol of preparing them for the new way of life that begins at baptism. The priest will use the oil to make the sign of the cross as a symbol of God's protective love for your children. The oil actually represents many things – it's very difficult to think of anything that means quite the same in our ordinary life. As well as protecting the child, the oil helps us to pay attention to everything that is holy and special about them as a completely unique individual with their own gifts and their own beauty. When the Queen was anointed with oil in her coronation service, it was such a special, holy moment that the cameras were not allowed to film it. *Invite someone to put the sun cream and the oil in the bag.*

Additional activity: We are all special

You will need:

- Olive oil.

  - o Invite everyone to think quietly for a few moments about the things that make them special.

  - o Invite them to use oil to draw a cross on the back of their own hands.

- **Water** (font): Water is one of the most basic and important things we need in life. It keeps us alive when we drink it, and we use it to keep ourselves clean and to refresh us. The water in the font reminds us of all these things. It also represents the idea that, at the moment of baptism, we are moving through the water from one way of life to another, just as we pass through the waters that break when we are born. We pass through the water as people in the Bible passed through the waters of the Red Sea on their way from slavery to freedom, and as Jesus passed through the waters of death and rose to new life. We also leave behind an old way of life when we are baptized; something dies and we rise to a new way of life in Christ. *Invite someone to put the bottle of water in the bag.*

Additional activity: Handwashing

You will need:

- A large bowl of water.
- A towel or roll of kitchen towels.
  - o Invite everyone to think quietly for a few moments about all the things they use water for every day.
  - o Invite them to wash their hands and then dry them.

- **Torch and candle** (the place where candidates are given a candle, e.g. the chancel step or by the Easter candle): We need light for our journey. At night, we might switch on our headlights or use a torch. If we wake up in the night feeling scared, perhaps because we have heard a strange noise, we are likely to turn on a light as soon as we can. Jesus said that he is the light of the world. Those who believe in him will never walk in darkness, but will have the light of life. However dark or difficult life is, we carry the light of Christ with us and it can show us the way forward. Your children will be given candles to remind them that they carry the light of Christ with them for the rest of their lives. *Invite someone to put the torch and candle in the bag.*

Additional activity: Light and dark

One of the earliest games children play is 'Peep-o!', hiding their eyes and then looking. One of the ideas they are exploring is what it means for us to be there or be absent. There is a bit of fear and danger in closing your eyes, and there is comfort and reassurance in opening them and finding that the person you love is still there. Invite people to close their eyes and put their hands over them for a few seconds and imagine what is going on in the room. How do they know everyone is still there? Invite them to open their eyes. How does it feel?

When we arrive at the end of the service, your children's bags will be packed with some of the most important things they will need on their journey through life.

Or

CHRISTENING GIFTS (10–15 MINS)

You will need:

- A bag or box containing the following items:
  o Passport.
  o Cross.
  o Water.
  o Candle.

Ask the families whether anyone has asked them to suggest christening gifts for their child. Make a list of the gifts they think would be suitable.

Explain that, during the baptism service in which their children will be christened, the children will receive some special gifts. Invite someone to have a 'lucky dip' in your bag and take out one of the items. Explain each item, using the following as a guide:

- **Passport**: God knew and loved your children before they were born, and they were legally named when you registered their birth. In baptism, they are named as children in God's family, which is why our first names are called 'Christian' names. Being christened or baptized is not something that happens and then we move on. Your children will be baptized children of God for ever, and their names are part of that identity.

- **Cross**: Your children will be marked with the sign of the cross. This is to remind us all that your children are holy in the sight of God and protected by the love of Jesus Christ. Your children will be marked for ever as followers of the way of Jesus.

- **Water**: The water we pour during the service reminds us of God's love and blessings flowing over your children on their special days and for the whole of their lives. Your children cannot go anywhere that God has not already been, and God's love will be with them wherever they may travel.

- **Candle**: With Jesus as part of their lives, your children will never walk in darkness, but will have the light of life. They will take that light with them as they carry their candles out of church and for the rest of their lives. Their baptism candles are there to remind them that they are to shine for Jesus.

The children will probably receive many other gifts and presents on their christening day, but these gifts that they are given during the service are very important for the rest of their lives.

PROMISES, PROMISES (10 MINS)

You will need:

- Three hoops or boxes.
- Copies of the promises from your church's baptism service (one for each person who can read).
- One copy of each promise in larger print on separate pieces of paper or card.

Very important promises are made in a baptism service. This simple activity encourages families to think about who is promising what and to whom. The research shows that churches are very concerned about whether people understand enough about what these promises mean and what they are committing themselves to. Churches need to appreciate that parents and godparents are far less concerned about having a complete intellectual understanding of the words they are saying. For them, the most important aspect of these promises is their commitment to do the very best for their child and to give them a good start in life.

Invite the families to think about promises they have made in their lives. For example, they might include marriage vows, Brownie or Cub promises, taking an oath in a court, the military oath of allegiance, or promises to repay a debt or do a job.

In the baptism service, parents, godparents and the congregation make some very important promises. Read through the promises together.

We make these promises:

- To God.
- To the child.
- To each other.

Put out the hoops or boxes and explain that one is for promises made to God, one is for promises made to the child, and the last one is for promises made to each other. Read out each promise from the separate pieces of paper or card and invite people to suggest which hoop or box to put them into.

You could invite parents and godparents to write a card to their child, making promises for their future lives (see below and photocopiable sheet 2.4, p. 102). If your families are making a memory book, the cards could be put into that.

Dear (child's name),

I promise that I will

With love from

WHAT HAPPENS WHEN

It is very important for families to have a clear idea of what will happen during the service, and particularly what they will be expected to do and say. The research found that this is the main thing they want from baptism preparation. They are likely to be more relaxed and engage fully at the service if they are not worried about what is going to happen next.

Give each family a copy of your church's order of service, or put up an outline of it on a screen or flipchart.

- Make sure the families know that they don't need to remember anything — the person leading the service will always make sure they are in the right place and know what to do.

- Assure them that you and the congregation are going to be delighted to welcome the whole family to the service, including the children, and that you are relaxed about children and their parents doing whatever they need to do to make the service a relaxed and happy occasion.

- Go through the order of service, drawing attention to the key elements that you covered in the previous activity.

- Invite questions.

7. CLOSING PRAYER (5–10 MINS)

Water for life, cleansing and refreshment

Water is at the heart of the baptism service. You could invite the parents to wash their hands as a reminder of their own baptisms (if they are baptized themselves) and as a way of preparing for the baptism of their child. You could ask them to think about whether there is anything in their life they would like to wash away from their lives as they prepare for this new start. If you are meeting in church, you might feel it is appropriate to wash hands in the font.

You could say the following prayer:

God, we thank you for the gift of water.
It quenches our thirst, gives us life, cleanses and refreshes us.
As we prepare for our children's baptisms, give us clean hearts.
In the name of your Son, Jesus Christ, who gives us the water of life. **Amen.**

Oil, water and light

If you used either of the Session 1 prayer activities using oil, water and light (see p. 58), you could either relight the lamps or repeat the second activity.

PRAYER CARD

Read a prayer together. You could light a candle before you begin.

Suggested prayers

Loving God,
we pray for your blessing on our family
as we prepare for the christening of our child.
Help us to follow Jesus together.
Amen.

Or this one from the website **www.churchofenglandchristenings.org/prayers**:

Creator God,
We thank you for the gift of the life of this child who is to be baptized.
May your blessing of peace and joy be with them
and protect them all of their days.
We make this prayer in the name of your Son, Jesus.
Amen.

SESSION 2: ADDITIONAL MATERIAL

These additional materials are an extra resource for you to use if you will have time to fill; or they could replace sections of the main material. For example, some groups may prefer to watch and discuss a film clip rather than using the activity in the section titled 'Welcome and introductions'.

1. FILM CLIP (10 MINS)

If you have the equipment to play film clips, show the scene from the end of *Toy Story 2* in which Jessie proudly shows everyone that Andy has written his name on her boot. Discuss the following questions:

- What does it mean for Jessie to have Andy's name on her boot?

- How will her life be different from now on?

- In the baptism service, we are marked with the cross, the sign of Christ, as members of God's family. What might this mean in our own lives and the lives of our children?

2. MAKE A CHRISTENING GIFT (20 MINS)

This activity would work particularly well in a session that used the 'Christening gifts' section (p. 88) to think about the key elements of the baptism service. Make sure you provide everything the families need to make their own gift to give their child at the service. The instructions here are for a christening mug or a candle, but you there are many other possibilities.

Christening mug

You will need:

- Plain white mugs (one for each child) – inexpensive mugs are best because the cheaper glazes usually keep the colours better. Suitable mugs are available from craft suppliers as well as homeware shops.

- Sharpie pens or craft pens for using on porcelain, pencils.

Give each family a plain white mug to decorate as a christening gift for their child, using the Sharpie pens or craft pens. Draw the designs on the mugs in pencil first and then colour in. The child's name would be a good focus for the decoration. If possible, allow the mugs to stand for at least 24 hours, then bake in a hot oven (230°C, Gas Mark 8 – put the mugs in when the oven is cold) for 45–60mins. There is still a chance that the designs will wash off in a dishwasher, so these mugs are for display rather than for using.

Baptism candle

> *You will need:*
>
> - Plain candles (one for each child)
> - Candle pens (available from craft suppliers and internet shops).

Give each family a plain white candle to decorate with symbols from the baptism service, e.g. cross, waves of water, the child's name.

3. GODLY PLAY (20 MINS)

Godly Play is an approach to Scripture and worship that encourages wondering together about a story, allowing each person to have their own response to it. Godly Play involves creating sacred space, offering the word of God, allowing those present (of whatever age) a free response, sharing a feast, and then going out into the world. This approach to story is deeply concerned with the possibility of encounter with God rather than the goal of learning about God. See **www.godlyplay.org.uk** for more information.

There is an excellent set of Godly Play resources for baptism,[6] and you could use these.

4. CLOTHED IN CHRIST (20 MINS)

Invite each person to name something that they hope for their child as they grow up.

Or, have a box of dressing-up clothes or a set of pictures representing what the children might want to be when they grow up, e.g. doctor (stethoscope), dancer (ballet shoes), astronaut (space helmet), pop star (microphone), footballer (football), neighbour (ordinary T-shirt), rich (money). Invite the families to choose one thing to represent their hopes for their child as they grow up.

---

[6] Jerome Berryman, *The Complete Guide to Godly Play: Volume 3*, Morehouse Education Resources, 2002.

At the baptism service, their children will set out into a new way of life, supported on their journey by their godparents, parents, and the church community. One reading from the Bible says something special about this new life.

Read Galatians 3.26–29. At the end, invite everyone to sit in silence for a few minutes. Discuss some or all of the following questions:

- This passage was written by Paul, a follower of Christ, to Christians living in Galatia between 40 and 60 AD. The passage tells us that when we find faith, we are free from the things that make us prisoners or slaves.

- What sort of things make people prisoners or slaves today? Examples could include addiction to alcohol, drugs or gambling, telling lies, spending too much time on the computer or phone.

- What would it mean to live a really full and happy life?

- Paul says that everyone who has been baptized has clothed themselves with Christ. The old barriers of race, gender and social status mean nothing when we are all one in Christ. What sort of world do we dream of for our children's future? How can being part of a church community help bring that dream to reality?

As a creative response, you could take a large piece of cloth (lining fabric would work well) and provide sequins, beads, buttons, tassels, etc., to decorate it. Invite people to choose an item to represent their own baptism and its place in their life and sew or pin them on. You could give each person a small piece of fabric to decorate and then attach the pieces to the cloth later. The finished robe could be used in baptism services in your church, perhaps being placed around each candidate immediately after they are baptized. Future families could be invited to add their own item to the decoration.

AND FINALLY ...

This second session covers the material that the majority of families most want information about. Many of them will have been anxious about what will happen in church during the baptism service and what will be expected of them. By the end of the session it is hoped they will be feeling more relaxed and confident about this.

They will have a clearer idea about the content of the service, having explored the meaning of the main symbols used and reflected on the promises that will be made. There isn't time to explain all of this during the service itself, so this time of preparation and thinking will help to make the service more significant, memorable and meaningful for the families.

PHOTOCOPIABLE MATERIAL
FOR SESSION 2

PHOTOCOPIABLE SHEET 2.1
TOPICS COVERED IN SESSION 1
(to use with 'Welcome and introductions', p. 81)

Christening and baptism.

Choosing names.

Getting ready for a baby.

Getting ready for a christening.

Who are godparents?

Why these godparents?

Prayer.

Oil, water, light.

PHOTOCOPIABLE SHEET 2.2
EXPERIENCE AND EXPECTATIONS GAME
Instructions (see p. 82)

EXPERIENCE AND EXPECTATIONS GAME

INSTRUCTIONS FOR ROLLING THE DICE

If you roll a ...	Name one thing that ...
1	... you like about church.
2	... you think churches could do better.
3	... you remember about the first time you went to church.
4	... you remember about the last time you visited a church.
5	... you are hoping for at your child's christening.
6	... you are worried about for your child's christening.

PHOTOCOPIABLE SHEET 2.3
TREASURE MAP
(to see with activity on p. 84)

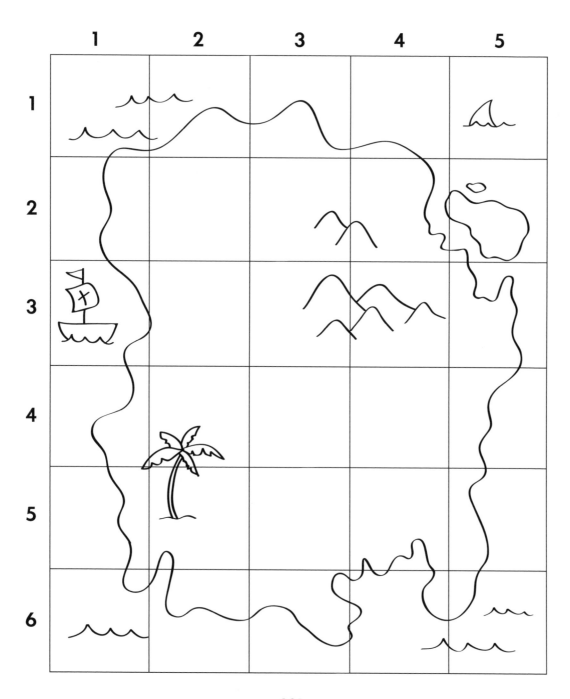

PHOTOCOPIABLE SHEET 2.4
PROMISES CARD
(see p. 91)

Dear (*child's name*),

I promise that I will

With love from

SESSION 3:
THE JOURNEY CONTINUES

THE AIM OF THE SESSION

In this final session, the family will think about their life together after the service and the place of faith within it. The families will probably be focusing on their plans for the christening day, but baptism is much more than a one-off event. These sessions are a good opportunity to help families prepare themselves for the months and years ahead, as their children grow up and begin to become independent adults. Humans are created as spiritual beings, with a deep sense of awe, wonder and mystery from a very young age.[7] This spiritual nurture is at the heart of the promises parents, godparents and congregations make in the baptism service. However, the role of parents in encouraging the fullest development of a child's spirituality receives very little attention in advice and literature about raising children, and most families have little experience or information on which to draw. Churches can play a key role in providing support and guidance in this area of life – it is absolutely central to what church is for.

This is your final session together, so you may choose to provide refreshments that make it feel like a party, e.g. cakes instead of biscuits, or ordering pizzas to be delivered to your building. The group will know each other reasonably well

---

[7] If you would like to find out more, Rebecca Nye's work *Children's Spirituality: What it is and why it matters*, CHP, 2009 is an excellent place to start.

by this stage and it would be good to relax and have some fun together. People who don't usually come to church are sometimes surprised to discover that parties and celebrations are an important part of church life!

Before the preparation course began, the top priority for most families will have been to find out what will happen in church on their child's christening day and what they will be expected to do and say. They will have received this information in Session 2, so it is important to give them strong reasons for wanting to return for Session 3. If the first two sessions have been helpful and engaging, and if the families have felt warmly welcomed and become part of the group, they are more likely to want to keep coming. Telling them that Session 3 includes a bit of a party could be an extra attraction.

As already stated, the focus of this session is on what happens *after* the christening day. At baptism, important promises are made and the whole family, including the godparents, set out on a new and exciting journey together as the child grows up. When children are young, it is impossible to imagine how family life will change over the years ahead. One of the texts in the commission section of the baptism service notes, 'As their parents and godparents, you have the prime responsibility for guiding and helping [this child] in their early years. This is a demanding task for which you will need the help and grace of God.'[8]

There is a wide range of advice and guidance available to parents as they prepare for the arrival of a child and in their earliest months and years, but there may be very little support to be found during a child's teenage years. As my own children have grown up, I have had less support from, for example, health visitors, NCT groups and family centres, and less contact with other parents from places such as playgroup and the school playground. Parents can feel isolated and anxious as their children become teenagers and young adults who are increasingly independent but nonetheless wrestling with a huge variety of issues and their own anxieties.

---

[8] *Common Worship: Christian Initiation*, Church House Publishing, 2005, p. 72.

In the baptism service, parents and godparents promise to walk with their children and support them as they grow up. These promises mean different things as the child develops. In the early years, there is an emphasis on protecting the child and providing the food, drink and comfort needed in order to survive and thrive. As time goes on, opportunities to learn and develop social skills and relationships become more important. As children enter adolescence, they need to learn how to be independent and begin to prepare for adult life, and this needs to happen within safe boundaries and at the right pace. Each child is, of course, unique, and every family has to work out for themselves how to negotiate these phases. Churches have a great deal to offer in supporting families at every stage. They can provide a listening ear, practical advice and support, and an awareness that the families are not alone, all underpinned by a commitment to prayer.

Baptism marks the beginning of a new phase in the family's spiritual life. Just as children develop physically, intellectually and emotionally, they also learn and grow spiritually. But there is much less awareness in society as a whole of the importance of spiritual development, and little knowledge among families about how to encourage and promote it. Very few of the parents and godparents I have met over the years have had any experience of prayer. Some will have heard prayers being said at school or at church, but they have rarely experienced prayer at home or been aware of praying themselves. The idea that prayer can be a significant part of family life is usually alien. This was true for both me and my husband. His family went to church, but never prayed at home. My family did neither. Developing some very simple (and fun!) prayers and prayerful rituals with our children became an important part of our identity as a family, and it has strengthened and deepened all of us.

Baptism preparation is a precious opportunity to explore with families how they might develop their own family spirituality and encourage their children to develop and flourish spiritually. To do this, they will need to be convinced that this is something worth doing that will enrich their family life. They will also need some simple suggestions of activities to try together.

During this final session, the families will:

- Think about the way children's needs change as they grow older. The role of parents changes enormously from the day the child arrives in the house to the day the young adult leaves home, and into the future beyond that.

- Remember special times they have already shared with their child and their importance in binding us to the people we love.

- Find out more about the support and activities your church offers families. You might also discover what families would like you to offer. It would be good to make sure that what you offer matches what families say they want and need.

- Explore ways of sharing Bible stories with children. Many parents know only a few core stories themselves, but many colourful books, puzzles, DVDs and internet resources are available that they could enjoy sharing with their children as they learn more of God's story together.

- Reflect on what prayer is and how to pray with and for children. Most parents have very little, if any, experience of prayer. They are likely to expect it to be difficult and something that only really good and holy people know how to do 'properly'. In fact, prayer can be very, very simple and it is something that anyone can do, at any time, in any place. And it can be fun!

THE JOURNEY MATTERS ...

... TO FAMILIES

Many families see their child's christening as the start of a journey of faith. They often express a desire for their children to know about God and about Christianity so that they can make their own decisions about religion as they grow up. This quote from one of the research families says it very well:

'One of the reasons for having our children christened was to give them a good foundation for faith. We ourselves aren't full-on religious people but we do attend church on special occasions and if our children decided to become devout Christians we would be fully supportive and feel we have made it easy for them to follow the faith if they choose to do this. Our christenings were really important for this, bringing our children in and introducing them to the church formally.'

... TO CHURCHES

When we welcome a new member into our family, we usually build a relationship with them over many months and years. We continue to take care of them and pay attention to them, inviting them to meals and parties, sending them cards, and making an effort to ensure that they start to feel that they belong. In a baptism service, we welcome a new member into the family of the church. Families often say they would like further contact from the church, but do not always expect to receive it. It would be good to find ways to build relationships with them in the same way as we would for new members of our own families.

Quotes from the research families illustrate the kind of church contact they would appreciate:

'It would be quite nice if you would have a newsletter or something like that. I thought they would hit quite regularly, I thought you would also get letters from the vicar, but not really, no. I would like to hear from them about any events that they're doing, and then anything that is for children, anything like that. But it would be too much if they would ask me to come along every week to service because that's just not, you know, when you got 2 children and husband's away from home, you can't go and spend all morning.'

'I don't think I've heard from them since the christening . . . it would have been nice to have a little reminder that they are still there.'

... TO GOD

After the resurrection, Jesus told his disciples to 'go and make disciples of all nations'. They would not be doing this alone because Jesus would be with them 'to the end of the age' (Matthew 28.18–20). Travelling in the company of Christ and of fellow pilgrims is a central idea in Christianity, which began as a movement called 'The Way'. Journeys are important in the Bible, from the story of Abraham to Paul's conversion and subsequent travels. God has known and loved the children being brought for baptism since before they were born, and will continue to accompany them in all the years ahead and through death itself. The christening day is a special moment within this journey and identifies the candidate as a baptized child of God from that day forward.

RUNNING SESSION 3: MAIN SESSION

Even if your other sessions were only an hour long, it would be good to allow at least one and a half hours for this final session, to allow plenty of time for chatting and sharing refreshments. This would work best at the end of the session, although you might still offer people a cup of tea or coffee when they arrive, particularly if they are coming straight from work.

1. SETTING UP BEFORE THE SESSION

It is still just as important to make sure everything is ready before people arrive, and that any issues that have come up in the first two sessions have been addressed.

CORE PROGRAMME OVERVIEW: SESSION 3

Arrival and Welcome	15 minutes
Introduction	5 minutes
The ups and downs of family life OR Talk about	10 minutes
What happens after the service	10 minutes
Praying with and for children	10 minutes
Sharing God's story	10 minutes
Closing prayer activity	5–10 minutes
	65 minutes plus discussion time

2. AS PEOPLE ARRIVE (10 MINS)

If everything has gone well in the previous sessions, families will know each other well enough to feel relaxed and comfortable. However, there may still be some new people attending for the first time and it is important to make sure they feel welcomed and become part of the group.

3. WELCOME AND INTRODUCTIONS (5 MINS)

You will need:

- A list of what was covered in Session 2 (see photocopiable sheet 3.1, p. 128).

- Marker pens or sticky coloured dots or stars.

Introduce all the people who are helping at the session – the leaders, those serving refreshments, and anyone else in the room. It would be good to wear name badges. You may have introduced yourselves already, but some people may not have been there and not everyone will remember.

Welcome the families and tell them how much you have enjoyed the last two sessions, how good it is to see them again (and to meet anyone who is new to the group), and how much you are looking forward to this session.

Display a large copy of the list of what was covered in Session 2.

Ask everyone to put a tick or a coloured dot or star next to the thing that sticks most in their minds from the last session.

Invite each person to find someone from another family (swapping seats if necessary) and to talk to them about which item on the list they ticked and why.

4. INTRODUCTION TO THE SESSION (5 MINS)

Explain that this is the last of three sessions. In the first session, we talked about getting ready for the christening day and the special role of godparents. Last time, we went through what happens in the service itself and what it means. In this session, we will begin to get ready for the months and years ahead. Say that you hope that this will make the service even more special and significant.

Remind everyone that everything said in the sessions should be treated as confidential to the group and not gossiped about. While everyone should feel able to be honest, this is not the right place to be pouring out heart and soul. Explain that people should only speak about things that they are happy for everyone in the group to know. (It is particularly important to spell this out again if there is anyone new to the group.)

5. THE UPS AND DOWNS OF FAMILY LIFE (10 MINS)

Choose one of these two activities; 'Simple board game' or 'Talk about'.

Simple board game

You will need:

- A copy of the board game and cards (see photocopiable sheet 3.2, pp. 129–135).

- Coloured counters or playing pieces to move on the board, a different colour for each family.

Print out the board game sheet and cards. Use different coloured paper or card for the three different stages of the game.

Divide the cards into three packs, one for each stage of the game. Place them face down, making sure you know which pack is for which stage.

Give each family a playing piece to represent a child in their care and line these pieces up along the bottom of the board, in the section named 'Birth – Start Here'.

Explain that this game is a simple way to think about some of the normal ups and downs of family life. Obviously, all children and families are different and will each do things in their own way, and this game is much more general than that. It is a simple way to have some fun while talking about the joys and challenges of being a family over the years ahead.

Invite one person from the first family to take a card from the 'Early Years' pile and follow the instructions. Then invite a person from the next family to take a turn.

When a family's counter or playing piece crosses a boundary into the next stage up or down, they need to take their next card from the pile for that stage.

Keep playing until one of the counters arrives in the final section at the end of the board, representing their children reaching the age of 18.

You could spend some time discussing what surprised people about the joys and challenges on the cards. What extra cards would they add?

Talk about

Invite people to give their answers to the following questions. If there are more than two or three families, it might be helpful to note the answers on a flipchart or screen.

- What do children need in order to flourish?

- How do these needs change as children grow older?

- How does the role of parents change as children grow older?

6. WHAT HAPPENS IN THE MONTHS AND YEARS AFTER THE SERVICE? (10 MINS)

In the family

Explain that whether you are a parent or godparent, friend or relative, spending time with children you know can be really special, and it's part of the amazing journey of faith. Just being together helps to grow strong relationships and helps children to discover more about other people. Discovery and imagination are part of what makes us unique humans. Wondering together at God's incredible world, laughing at fun things and learning how to get over mistakes are all important aspects of life after the christening.

- Ask people to say a few words about a special moment or time they have shared with their child. In a larger group, people might talk in smaller groups or pairs. How did it make them feel to remember it?

- Remind people that these special memories are part of what binds us together in loving relationships.

- Explain that there are suggestions of things to do together on the website at **www.churchofenglandchristenings.org/after-a-christening/days-fun-times.**

- Encourage families to sign up for the e-newsletter, Next Steps, at **www.churchofenglandchristening.org**.

With the church

Background for session leaders: Families often say that they would like to have more contact with the church after their child's baptism. During the service, the congregation promises to welcome and uphold the candidate in their new life in Christ.

It is important for you to remember in these conversations that many adults are anxious about coming to church because they don't know what will be expected of them and they worry about 'getting things wrong'. In addition, parents are often anxious about bringing children to church in case they disturb others. They may also be concerned that having come once they will be expected to come every week, which is not possible for a lot of people. Simply coming to a church fair or coffee morning may be quite a daunting step for some families. If they feel warmly welcomed and are invited to other events, these small steps can become significant in a family's spiritual journey.

- Ask the families to suggest ways in which they would like the church to keep in touch with them. What sort of events and services might they be interested in? You may not be able to follow up all the ideas, but you can promise to listen carefully, and include them in your planning.

- This is a good opportunity to let people know what provision your church makes for children at services and other activities, including community events, and also to explain any arrangements for ongoing contact.

- Invite questions.

7. PRAYING WITH AND FOR CHILDREN (10 MINS)

You will need:

- Map of your community that can be opened up on the floor.
- Sticky notes.
- Pens or pencils.

Explain that there are many different ways of praying, just as there are many different methods of communicating with other people. Some prayers are written down in formal language; others may be shorter than a tweet. Some prayers do not use words at all, but are prayed through pictures, in music, or with our hearts and souls. There are no right or wrong words to use. Prayer is about spending time in God's company offering our thanks, worries, loved ones, or difficult situations into God's love and light, trusting in God's promise to hear us when we call upon him.

Praying for and with our children is one of the most important things we can do. In our prayers, we are treasuring them within the love and light of God, paying deep attention to the beauty and wonder of the people God created our children to be. This can be as simple as lighting a candle (see the christenings website, **www.churchofenglandchristenings.org/light-candle-2**), or saying 'God, I pray for (*child's name*),' perhaps while looking at a photo of the child. There are more suggestions at **www.churchofenglandchristenings.org/after-a-christening/prayer**.

Praying with children could include reading from books of children's prayers, saying a simple prayer together at bedtime, giving thanks before meals (saying grace), or saying the words, 'May God bless you and keep you', to your child whenever you say goodbye. As children grow older, you could invite them to add their own words when you pray. It is worth keeping a notebook in the place where you pray to record things your child says that you want to remember.

Lay out the map of your community. Ask everyone to write the name of their child on a sticky note. Walk round the map together and invite people to place their sticky notes on a place that is important to their child. It might for example be their home, the venue for a toddler group, a doctor's surgery, or a playground.

Invite people to think quietly about what they might want to say to God while their child is in that particular place. It might, for example, begin, 'Thank you, God, for ...' or, 'Please, God, take care of my child while ...' Ask if anyone is happy to share their prayer.

8. SHARING GOD'S STORY (10 MINS)

You will need:

- A set of pictures representing some very well-known Bible stories (you can download them from the internet — see below for list).

- The title for each story – print the list and cut out the titles (see photocopiable sheet 3.3, p. 136).

- Sticky tac.

- A collection of children's Bible resources, e.g. storybooks, children's Bibles, sticker books, books of puzzles and activities, DVDs, list of internet resources.

- Sticky dots or stars.

Display a set of pictures of some of the best-known Bible stories. The list below includes the most familiar titles. You can find free clipart pictures for them on the internet.

LIST OF BIBLE STORIES

Adam and Eve in the Garden of Eden

Noah's ark

Moses leads the people of Israel through the Red Sea

David and Goliath

Jonah and the whale

Daniel in the lions' den

Jesus is born

The Good Samaritan

Jesus heals a man lowered through the roof

Jesus meets Zacchaeus

Jesus meets the woman at the well

Jesus goes to the home of Mary and Martha

Jesus dies on the cross

The women find Jesus' tomb is empty

The Holy Spirit comes

St Paul meets Christ on the road to Damascus

Invite each person to take the title of one story and stick it on the picture they think it matches.

When they have done this, you could give them another story title, if there are any left.

Explain that the Bible includes stories, histories, poetry, guidance on good ways to live, letters, warnings, promises and dreams.

Explain that the Bible is not a single book. It contains 66 books in different styles: some are poetry, some history, others are letters.

Explain that many resources are available for families that will help them find out more about the contents of the Bible. Look through the collection you have brought. If you have a local Christian bookshop, they may be happy to organize a display of items on a 'sale or return' basis. You may want to buy something appropriate for each family.

Give each person a coloured dot or star.

Invite them to stick it on the story they like best.

Read the story that has the most coloured dots from one of the children's Bibles you have brought.

9. CLOSING PRAYER

Light

Light is the final great symbol of the baptism service. At the end of the service candidates are given a candle and sent out to live in the light of Christ and to shine as lights in the world to the glory of God the Father. You could invite the families to light the children's own baptism candles, the ones that will be used in the service. If your church has a large Easter candle, it would be good to light the children's candles from this. If not, light them all from a single large candle. As you light this large candle, you could ask the parents to think about anything in their own lives that makes them feel afraid, sad, or a bit lost. Invite them to ask God to shine his light into these things to give them strength and courage.

As you light the children's candles, you could say the following prayer:

We thank you, God, for the gift of light.
It helps us find the way through life.
We pray that this light may give us strength and courage.
May we walk in the light of Christ as we prepare for the baptism of our children and in the months and years ahead.

May we and our children shine as lights in the world
to the glory of God the Father. **Amen.**

Oil, water and light

If you used either of the Session 1 prayer activities using oil, water and light in
the previous sessions you could either relight the lamps or repeat the second
activity (see p. 60).

Prayer card

Read the prayer below together (or another suitable prayer). You could light
a candle before you begin.

Loving God,
we pray for your blessing on our family
as we prepare for the christening of our child.
Help us to walk together in the Way of Christ.
Amen.

SESSION 3: ADDITIONAL MATERIAL

These additional materials are an extra resource to use as required. Some of
them could replace sections of the main material. For example, some groups
may prefer to watch and discuss a film clip rather than using the activity in the
section titled 'Welcome and introductions'.

1. FILM CLIP (10 MINS)

If you have the equipment to play film clips, show one that includes people
setting out into a different phase of life. A child's baptism is the beginning
of a new stage of their life. Their parents and godparents, and the church
congregation, make important promises to care for them in a new way. The sort
of care a child needs changes as they grow up and it would be good to choose

a film clip that explores this idea. For example, you could show the scene near the beginning of *Finding Nemo* (U) in which Marlin is taking Nemo for his first day of school and is very anxious about leaving him. You could discuss with the families how they feel about their children growing up and becoming more independent. After this discussion, you could show a clip from the end of the film, where after all their adventures Marlin takes Nemo back to school.

2. A FAMILY HOME (10–15 MINS)

You will need:

- A large picture of the floor plan of a house or flat typical of your area (there are plenty of images online if you enter 'floor plan' into the images section of a search engine).

- Sticky notes in two colours.

- Pens or pencils.

The main focus of this session is on the months and years ahead in the life of the child and their family. In this activity, people are invited to think about the impact of the arrival of a new child and the changes that take place as the child grows up and develops. These changes are reflected in all sorts of ways in the child's home. Over the years, the changing mat and toy collection are replaced by teenagers' toiletries and digital equipment.

Ask people to think about how their home has changed since the arrival of their child. For example, there will probably be a pile of toys somewhere, and they may have had to rearrange who sleeps where.

Invite them to think about each of the following spaces and write or draw on a sticky note something that has changed in that area of the home:

- Living area.

- Kitchen.

- Bedrooms.

- Bathroom.

Put the sticky notes in the relevant places on the floor plan.

Now give people sticky notes in a different colour. Ask them to imagine what will be different in each area of the home when their child is a teenager. Invite them to write or draw these on the sticky notes and add them to the floor plan.

Discuss how children's needs change as they grow up. This will affect the running of the family home and the relationships between the people who live there. In the end, most children will leave home when they are grown up. One of the most important tasks parents have is to build relationships with their children that support them as well as possible at each stage of their development until they become independent adults. (Quentin Blake's book Zagazoo[9] illustrates this in a light-hearted way.)

During the baptism service, the congregation will promise to uphold the child as they grow up. Tell everyone that they and their children will be in your church's prayers at every stage of family life. Explain your church's arrangements for people to make contact with any prayer requests or to raise pastoral issues, for example if a parent or child is taken into hospital, a couple is going through a difficult time, or if a family would like to arrange a wedding or a funeral. If you have a church-based playgroup or school, you could explain the connections. If you remember baptism anniversaries in your church prayers, it would be good to mention this.

3. LIGHT FOR THE JOURNEY (10 MINS)

You will need:

- Pictures of different sources of light, or items to represent them, e.g. torch, traffic light, sun, lighthouse, star, light bulb, candle.

---

[9] Quentin Blake, Zagazoo, Red Fox, 2000.

Explain that the child will be given a lit candle at the end of the church service. This represents the idea that they will take the light of Christ with them when they leave the church building.

Explain that Jesus said he was the light of the world, and read John 8.12: 'Again Jesus spoke to them, saying, "I am the light of the world. Whoever follows me will never walk in darkness but will have the light of life."'

Ask people to look at the different sources of light and to suggest times when they might find them helpful. For example, a torch can help us find our way in the dark or to look for things we have lost under the sofa. A traffic light tells us when it is safe to keep going and when we need to stop. A lighthouse warns of danger and helps ships find a safe direction to move in. The sun helps us to keep warm and healthy. Turning on a light bulb can make us feel better when we are scared. A candle is useful when all other sources of power and light fail.

Invite people to reflect for a short time of quiet, thinking about how Jesus might be like one or two of these sources of light in different situations.

Invite each person to choose one of the pictures or objects and then to say a few words about the reasons for their choice.

4. MAKE A PRAYER CUBE OR CHATTERBOX (10 MINUTES)

You will need:

- Templates to cut out, fold and stick together to make a cube or chatterbox (see photocopiable sheets 3.4 and 3.5, pp. 137–8).

- Scissors.

- Glue.

- Books of children's prayers or sheets with simple prayers printed onto them.

- Coloured pens.

Invite the families to think about what things they would like to pray for and with their children.

Ask them to write a short prayer on each of the six faces of the cube or each section of the chatterbox. They may like to use the books or sheets of prayers to get them started.

Cut out the template and stick together to make a cube, or cut and fold to make a chatterbox.

Encourage the families to roll the cube or open the chatterbox each day and read the prayer for their child. You could give them spare templates to make new cubes or chatterboxes when the first one gets too tatty.

5. MAKE A PRAYER CARD (5 MINS)

You will need:

- Printed card for each family (see photocopiable sheet 3.6, p. 139)
- Coloured pens.

Give each person a printed card.

Invite them to write in their child's name, decorating each letter.

If your families are making a memory book, the cards could be added to that.

6. PHOTO TO TREASURE (5 MINS)

You will need:

- A photo frame that will hold two photos for each family, or two small photo frames.

Give each family a photo frame (to be taken away). Suggest that the family adds a photo from the child's christening day into one of the slots or frames.

In the other side or frame, suggest that they add another photo of the child, which they can then update each year on the anniversary of the christening service. This would be a good opportunity to think back over the last year, remembering good times and difficult times and reflecting on where God has been in the life of the family.

Over time, the difference between the photos will naturally increase as the child grows older, and the pictures will remind the family of the ways in which life has moved on.

7. CHRIST WITH US FOR THE JOURNEY (20 MINS)

Our journey through life is likely to include difficult and painful times as well as times of joy and peace. At these times, we need people who care about us and support us, walking alongside us, who know when we need to speak and when we need to listen, and when sharing silence is more meaningful than any words. In the story of the Good Samaritan, the wounded traveller is helped by a very unexpected person – someone he normally wouldn't have wanted to talk to. Jesus used this story to show people that they should always help and support those in need, even their enemies and be able to accept help from them too.

In the baptism service, parents, godparents and congregations promise to support the child as they grow up. Sometimes this will be a wonderful, joyful thing to do. At other times of the child's life, it may be a great challenge to know how best to help them. The most important thing is that the child is surrounded by people who love them and who have promised to support them through good times and bad.

Read the story of the Good Samaritan (Luke 10.25–37). This is included in many children's Bibles. There is a very simple version with excellent illustrations in *Stories Jesus Told* by Nick Butterworth and Mick Inkpen[10]. The Godly Play

---

[10] Nick Butterworth and Mick Inkpen, *Stories Jesus Told*, Candle Books, 2005.

materials include a very good telling of this story[11], or you could use the creative telling outlined below:

You will need:

- Brown ribbon, cloth, or paper to represent the road.

- Ribbons, strips of cloth or paper in the following colours: red, purple, black.

- Bandage.

- Two coins.

Read the script below, using the actions in italics as you go through the story.

Roll out the brown ribbon, cloth or paper to represent the road. 'Walk' the first two fingers of one hand along the road, to represent the traveller.

One day, a man was travelling from Jerusalem to Jericho.

On the way, robbers attacked him.

Take away your fingers and replace them with the red cloth.

They stripped him, beat him and left him for dead.

Pause.

A priest happened to be travelling along the road.

Drag the purple ribbon, cloth or paper along the road.

He saw the wounded man, but he passed by on the other side.

Drag the purple around the red, carefully avoiding it.

Next, a lawyer came along the road.

Drag the black ribbon, cloth or paper along the road.

---

[11] Jerome Berryman, *The Complete Guide to Godly Play: Volume 3*, Morehouse Education Resources, 2002.

But he also passed by on the other side.

Drag the black around the red, carefully avoiding it.

But then a Samaritan saw the wounded man. The people from Samaria were enemies of the people from Jerusalem, but this Samaritan's heart was moved with pity.

He bandaged the traveller's wounds.

Take away the red, and put the bandage in its place.

He put the wounded traveller on his own animal.

Turn one hand upside down so that all your fingertips touch the road, representing the Samaritan's animal. Make a fist with your other hand and rest it on top to represent the wounded traveller riding on the animal.

He took the man to an inn.

'Walk' your two hands along the road and then stop and take your top hand off, laying it down with the back of your hand next to the road.

He took care of him.

Use your free hand to stroke the one lying next to the road.

The next day, he gave the innkeeper two coins.

Lay down the two coins next to the hand lying next to the road.

He told the innkeeper to look after the man until he came back, and promised to repay any extra costs.

Pause.

Sit back and take both your hands away.

Invite everyone to sit in silence for a few minutes. Discuss some or all of the following questions:

- Who was the true neighbour to the man who was robbed?

- How might the man have felt when he saw a priest coming?

- How might he have felt when the priest passed by?

- How might he have felt when someone started to help him?

- How might he have felt when he realized his helper was a Samaritan?

- Have you ever been helped by an unlikely person?

- Which person in the story would we like our children to be like?

- How can we help them to grow up to be like that?

AND FINALLY ...

This is the last preparation session and the families will now be sorting out their final arrangements for the christening day. The aim of this session is to help them discover that baptism is more than a one-off event and to begin to prepare themselves for the months and years ahead.

The first two sessions covered a lot of material that families would already be familiar with from their experience of having a baby and planning the christening. This session introduces some things that may be completely new to them. Few new families can imagine what it will be like to have teenagers in their homes, and every child will be unique and special. The focus here is on ways families can make sure that they adapt to the child's changing needs as they grow up, and on ways of encouraging the child's spiritual development, as well as supporting their physical and emotional needs. It is also important to say that this can be fun, building a shared set of memories of happy times together, and paying attention to the life and beauty we can find all around us in God's amazing creation.

We hope that you have enjoyed getting to know the families and have built relationships with them that will continue to grow and deepen at the children's baptism services and in the years to come. It is important to keep them in your prayers and to keep in touch with them.

PHOTOCOPIABLE MATERIAL
FOR SESSION 3

PHOTOCOPIABLE SHEET 3.1
TOPICS COVERED IN SESSION 2
(to use with 'Welcome and introductions', p. 110)

Expectations of church

What church is like

The Bible

The service

Friends and family

Oil

Water

Candle

Gifts

Promises

Prayer

What we do in the service

What we say in the service

PHOTOCOPIABLE SHEET 3.2
THE UPS AND DOWNS OF FAMILY LIFE
Board game and cards (see p. 111)

	YOUR CHILD IS 18!
SECONDARY SCHOOL	
PRIMARY SCHOOL	
EARLY YEARS	
	BIRTH *START HERE*

Your baby smiles for
the first time.

Move forward 2 squares

While changing your
baby's nappy, he/she
is sick all over you.

Move back 1 square

Your baby sits
without support.

Move forward 1 square

Your child takes
his/her first step.

Move forward 2 squares

Your child can crawl!
Take time out to find
the stair gates.

Miss 1 turn

It's your child's
christening day.

Move forward 2 squares

Teething is making your
child restless. You haven't
slept for two nights.

Go back one square

There's an artist in the
family – and he/she has
used lipstick to decorate
the bathroom walls.

Miss 1 turn while you clean up

Your child says
his/her first word.

Move forward 1 square

When you clap your hands,
your child claps back.

Move forward 1 square

Your child jumps up and
down, both feet off the
ground.

Move forward 1 square

Your child points at
something and says,
'Look!'

Move forward 1 square

Your child no longer
needs nappies.

Move forward 2 squares

Your child no longer
needs nappies.

Move forward 1 square

Your child waves when
you say goodbye.

Move forward 1 square

Your child gives you
a big hug.

Move forward 1 square

It's the first day of school!

Move forward 2 squares

You have a friend of
your child round to play
and everything goes well.

Move forward 1 square

You have a friend round
to play, but your child tells
you to send them home.

Move back 1 square

You go out for a meal
and everyone sits and
eats and chats nicely
for the whole time.

Move forward 1 square

Your child brings in a
flower and tells you to
look carefully –
'Look at all the patterns.'

Move forward 1 square

You are out in the
evening and your child
asks why the stars shine.

Move forward 2 squares

Your child yells, 'I hate you!'

Move back 1 square

Your child gives you
a big hug.

Move forward 2 squares

There are nits in the classroom. It takes ages to check your child.

Miss 1 turn

The stomach bug that's been going round school comes home.

Miss 1 turn

Your child's teacher phones to tell you he/she is not happy at school and asks whether there are any problems at home.

Go back 1 square

Your child writes his/her first story.

Go forward 1 square

You struggle with your child's maths homework.

Miss 1 turn while you work it out

You have a wonderful sunny day together at the seaside.

Move forward 1 square

One of your child's godparents takes him/her out for the day.

Move forward 1 square

Your child falls off a swing and breaks an arm.

Go back one square

It's the first day of secondary school.

Move forward 2 squares

It's your child's last day at school.

Move forward 2 squares

Your child has a boyfriend/girlfriend.

Miss 1 turn while you work out how you feel about this

At parents' evening, you are told that your child is always polite and helpful.

Move forward 1 square

Your child does better than you were hoping in his/her exams.

Move forward 1 square

Your child has shut themselves in their bedroom and says they never want to speak to you again.

Move back 1 square

Your child gives you a big hug.

Move forward 2 squares

The school phones to tell you they are worried about your child. Friends say your child may be self-harming.

Move back 2 squares

It's pay day! Your child brings home their first earnings.

Move forward 1 square

Your child puts his/her clothes away without being reminded.

Move forward 1 square

Your child makes his/her own sandwiches for school.

Move forward 1 square

Dinner time – and your child has cooked it!

Move forward 1 square

You have a lovely day together at the seaside.

Move forward 1 square

You go out for a meal together without anyone complaining or using a phone at the table.

Move forward 1 square

Your find a pile of dishes in your child's room – and they are growing many colours of mould.

Move back 1 square

Your child loses his/her shoes – again.

Miss a turn while you look for them

LIST OF BIBLE STORIES

Adam and Eve in the Garden of Eden

Noah's ark

Moses leads the people of Israel through the Red Sea

David and Goliath

Jonah and the whale

Daniel in the lions' den

Jesus is born

The Good Samaritan

Jesus heals a man lowered through the roof

Jesus meets Zacchaeus

Jesus meets the woman at the well

Jesus goes to the home of Mary and Martha

Jesus dies on the cross

The women find Jesus' tomb is empty

The Holy Spirit comes

St Paul meets Christ on the road to Damascus

PHOTOCOPIABLE SHEET 3.4
TEMPLATE FOR PRAYER CUBE
(to be used with 'Make a prayer cube or chatterbox', p.121)

PHOTOCOPIABLE SHEET 3.5
TEMPLATE FOR A CHATTERBOX
(to be used with 'Make a prayer cube or chatterbox', p.121)

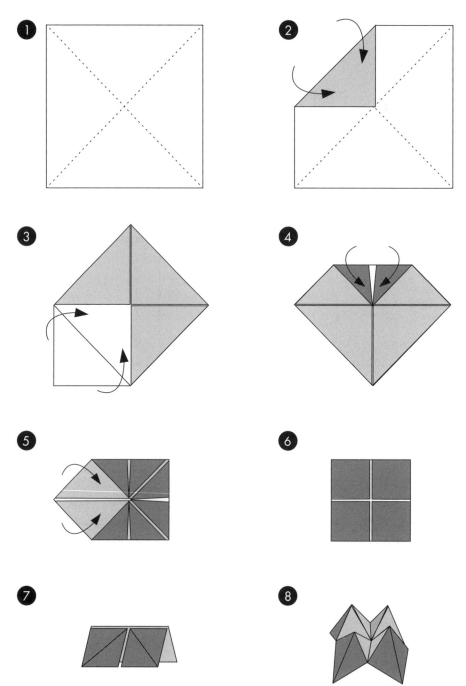

Loving God,

I pray for

(space for child's name)

Surround them with love and help them know more about your love for them every day.

Amen.

SINGLE SESSION WITH A GROUP

Although three sessions really help to build relationships with families and allow space to explore all that baptism can mean for a family, it is not always possible either for a church to offer or for a family to attend three sessions. It may be that there are not enough families, or perhaps so many that you would have to offer the programme more frequently than is practical. This section outlines a session that can be used on a single evening/afternoon with two or more families. It is a great opportunity for families to discover that there are others on the same journey as they are. They may already know each other from nursery, NCT classes or just around the community, or this may be an opportunity for them to meet others at the same stage of life as they are. Young parents can feel isolated, even lonely, and friendships forged with others in the same situation can last for years.

The material should take around 1 hour 30 minutes to deliver, but you should leave ample time for conversations and chat, so a typical session might last around two hours. This could take place in the evening or at a weekend, for example at about 3pm on a Saturday or Sunday. If you hold a session on a weekend afternoon you are more likely to get siblings coming along as well, so be prepared to involve toddlers and others or have activities for them to enjoy. You may like to hold a separate or additional rehearsal time where the focus is on the mechanics of the service – when to stand, what to say and so on. This means that you can use this session to focus on parents' expectations and to explore the meaning and purpose of baptism.

1. SETTING UP BEFORE THE SESSION

First impressions really do matter and it is important to get everything ready before course participants start to arrive. If you and your team are relaxed and confident as you welcome everyone, this will help others to relax too. Make your meeting space as tidy, comfortable and welcoming as possible (see p. 38 for more details).

- Prepare the refreshments.
  - o Provide a choice of tea, coffee, decaffeinated coffee and cold drinks.
  - o Home-made cakes and biscuits are always popular if you can arrange this.
  - o It is good hospitality to have gluten-free options available.
  - o Some families will appreciate the option of fruit for any children.
  - o If children are coming, make sure you have cups appropriate to their age range, e.g beakers with lids for toddlers.
  - o It is sensible to have some kitchen towels, baby wipes or cloths available in case of accidents or sticky fingers.
  - o Provide name badges for everyone, including yourself and your team.
  - o Colourful lanyards with plastic holders for name cards will make it easy to identify your team and are available at reasonable price on the internet.
  - o Sticky labels will be fine for the families.
- Look through the 'You will need' list for each of your chosen activities and make sure you have everything.

CORE PROGRAMME OVERVIEW: SINGLE SESSION WITH A GROUP

Arrival phase	10 minutes
Welcome and introduction	5 minutes
Overview	5 minutes
Starting the journey	5–10 minutes
Parents, grandparents, godparents	10–15 minutes
Christening gifts	10–15 minutes
The way we do things here	15 minutes (or separate rehearsal at church)
Tools for the journey	10 minutes
Directions and help	5–10 minutes
Sharing God's story	5–10 minutes
Closing prayer activity	5 minutes
	75–90 minutes

2. AS PEOPLE ARRIVE (10 MINS)

You will need:

- Pictures or cards with words to represent activities families enjoy. Make sure the activities represented are relevant in your context and the sort of things families there actually do together.

- Some blank cards and pens so that families can add their own choice of activities.

Families are likely to be anxious when they arrive. Some or all of these questions may be running through their minds:

- What is going to happen?

- Will there be difficult questions?

- If they don't know the 'right' answers, will their child still be christened?

- Will they have anything in common with the other people coming, or will they feel out of place?

- Do they need to be extra polite in front of church people?

- If their child(ren) are coming, will they behave?

A warm welcome to each person will help families begin to relax. These suggestions may help:

- Make sure that your church team is easy to identify (e.g. with colourful lanyards and name badges).

- Ask one of your team to stand at the door to invite people in and make sure they know where to collect refreshments and where to sit.

- Serve refreshments as people arrive. It can be a real challenge for families with young children to arrive at a precise time. There will almost always be an early arrival and some late ones. Chatting over refreshments is a good way to begin to build relationships and allows people to arrive comfortably over a period of time.

- Introduce families to each other as they arrive. Some of them may already know one another.

- Invite them to complete a name badge and have some activities for them to look at. You might like to create a photo board with pictures of things that take place at church, including family services and other baptisms (with the families' permission).

- Make sure you have toys and activities for children, as appropriate.

- Put the picture cards and blank cards out on a table or the floor in the middle of the group, together with pens. As families arrive, ask each of them to choose a card representing something they enjoy doing together.

If they have an idea that isn't on a card, ask them to take a blank one and represent their own idea. Leaders and helpers should take a card too.

Aim to begin formally within 10–15 minutes of your advertised start time. By then, hopefully, everyone should have arrived and found the refreshments. Move around the group and invite people to come and sit down in the circle of chairs, bringing the card(s) they have chosen with them. Make sure they are all sitting comfortably and that any babies and children have the things they need to be as happy as possible.

3. WELCOME AND INTRODUCTIONS (5 MINS)

At the start of the session, it is important to make sure everyone has a chance to learn other people's names and find out a bit about each other. The first activity is based on the cards that have been chosen and should give families a chance to begin to chat about something safe and familiar.

But first, let all those who are helping make brief introductions. This includes those serving refreshments, helpers and anyone else present. Encourage them to say something about an activity their family enjoys doing together. Then introduce yourself, explaining why you are leading the session (for example, because you are the vicar or because you are the organizer for all the baptism preparation in your area). Share the card you have chosen and the activity that your family enjoy together.

Then welcome the families and tell them how delighted you are that they have chosen to have their children baptized at a christening. This is a good moment to explain that the two words mean the same thing – but that the whole day is usually called the christening, and the church uses the word baptism to describe the moment when the water is poured on the child. During the session you will be telling them more about this and the other things that happen in the church as part of their special day.

Explain that you are going to invite each family to introduce themselves by giving their names (including their child or children) and saying which card they have chosen and why. Some families will be very confident in doing this, others will be very anxious.

When everyone has spoken, even if it's just two families, you and a helper, repeat how pleased you all are to be sharing in such a special day.

4. OVERVIEW OF THE SESSION (5 MINS)

It is important for people to have a general overview of what is going to be covered and to be clear about any 'ground rules', including confidentiality.

Explain that during the session you are going to think about how the baptism is like the start of a journey. Everybody will get a chance to think about why they started the journey, who is involved, what happens at the service and what difference it will make to the future. There may be other opportunities for families to discover more – don't forget to mention that they are welcome to come along to church services at any time.

Invite the families to ask any questions, and say that they can ask questions at any point during the session. Also let them know who to contact if they have questions afterwards.

Make it clear that everything said in the sessions should be treated as confidential to the group and not gossiped about. Emphasize that while everyone should feel that they can be honest, this is not the right place to be pouring out heart and soul. People should only speak about things that they are happy for everyone in the group to know.

Check whether anyone has any questions and then tell the group that you are going to move on to the first part of the session.

5. STARTING THE JOURNEY? (5–10 MINS)

You will need:

- A list of reasons that people might have for setting off on a journey (see below).

- A list of reasons why people might be having a christening (see below).

- A timer.

- Pens.

If you have a group of about twelve or more you might like to split into two teams for fun. The idea is the same.

Appoint one person from each team as the list holder – or if doing as one group, give the lists to a helper.

Give up to two minutes for people to call out as many answers as they can think of to the statement: 'reasons for setting off on a journey.'

Then repeat with 'reasons for deciding to have a christening.'

The idea is that they are trying to guess the reasons already on the list.

The winner is the team who guesses the most answers that are on the list.

REASONS FOR STARTING A JOURNEY

- **Need to earn a living**

- **Change of scene**

- **Feel lonely**

- **Children need to be occupied**

- **Want to spend time with partner**

- **Get fit or keep fit**

- Invitation from a friend

- Family need to eat

- Have fun

- Time to yourself

- Responsibility to others

- Somebody needs you

REASONS FOR DECIDING TO HAVE A CHRISTENING

- Family always have children christened

- Partner/family want it to happen

- Saying thank you for birth of a child

- Having godparents

- Becoming part of the church family

- Protection through life

- Making a good start in life

- To make sure there is a place in heaven for a child

- Having a party with family and friends

- Starting a journey of faith for a child

- Blessing for a child

- Friends are doing the same

Explain that we set off on journeys for a wide range of reasons, and deciding to have a child christened can be for all kinds of reasons too. The lists represent a selection of the reasons parents gave in a recent research project that was done. The important thing seemed to be that it is the beginning of something – the beginning of a journey. And people are an important part of any journey.

6. PARENTS, GRANDPARENTS, GODPARENTS (10–15 MINS)

> *You will need:*
>
> - A flipchart or flipchart-sized pieces of paper.
>
> - Marker pens.

Ask the families to suggest some of the people they expect will be important in the lives of their children down the years: siblings, grandparents, aunts and uncles, friends. Maybe godparents will be mentioned, which leads to the next discussion and activity.

Godparents are very important. They are chosen especially to be part of the journey that starts with the baptism at a christening.

Parents think very carefully before choosing people they trust to take a special interest in their child, act as good role models and play an important part in the life of the family for many years ahead. Churches also take the role of godparents very seriously, which is why there are some rules and guidelines about who can be a godparent when a child is baptized. You can find advice about this at **www.churchofenglandchristenings.org/for-parents/ choosing-godparents**.

It is good practice for churches to make the requirements clear at a very early stage of the enquiry, so that families are aware of them before this preparation session. This is a good opportunity to check whether the families have any questions. In particular, it may be worth checking that the people they have in mind do meet these requirements. If necessary, you may need to discuss this at a separate time with any families whose situation is complicated.

It is also worth making ensure that people understand the difference between godparents and legal guardians. There is widespread confusion about the role of godparents if anything should happen to the child's parents. Being a godparent is not the same as being a legal guardian. It may be helpful to point out that if families choose as godparents people they would like to take care of their children should the need arise, they should also appoint them as legal guardians in their wills.

Then give families time to talk about the following questions.

- Who have you chosen as godparents?

- Why have you chosen these people?

- What are you hoping they will do over the years?

Good godparents can help build solid foundations for a child's life.

Invite families to draw brick shapes on the flipchart paper and write on each brick something they think will be a good quality that a godparent will bring to their child and their family. Examples of qualities families are looking for might include:

- A good role model.

- Listens.

- Shows generosity.

- Makes time for them.

- Prays.

- Takes them to church.

- Shows kindness.

After people have finished listing the various qualities, draw the discussion together by explaining that in the service godparents promise to help support the child and the family as they discover what it means to be a Christian. You might like to read the four points from the greetings card for godparents (search **www.churchprinthub.org** for baptism resources). If you are going to use these cards, now might be a good time to give them to the parents to send to the godparents they have chosen.

Over the years to come, you'll help us on this journey by:

- *Being there for our child to talk to about the bigger questions of life.*

- *Praying for our child through the ups and downs of their faith journey.*

- *Showing them how to make good choices in life, for themselves and for others.*

- *Helping them to learn more about the Christian faith, through their church and in other ways.*

7. STARTING THE JOURNEY

The baptism service itself is at the heart of the day: like a wedding ceremony is at the heart of a wedding day.

Families are often anxious that they might not 'get things right'. So it will be really important to them that someone can run through the service with them.

The activity 'Christening gifts' should be adapted to reflect baptism practice in your church, and ideally supported by a time for rehearsal which includes the promises.

CHRISTENING GIFTS (10–15 MINS)

You will need:

- A bag or box containing the following items:

  o Passport.

  o Cross.

  o Water.

  o Candle.

  o A cheque book.

Ask the families whether anyone has asked them to suggest christening gifts for their child. Make a list of the gifts they think would be suitable.

Explain that, during the baptism service in which their children will be christened, the children will receive some special gifts. Invite someone to have a 'lucky dip' in your bag and take out one of the items. Explain each item, using the following as a guide:

- **Passport**: God knew and loved your children before they were born, and they were legally named when you registered their birth. In baptism, they are named as children in God's family, which is why first names are called 'Christian' names. Being christened or baptized is not something that happens and then we move on. Your children will be baptized children of God for ever, and their names are part of that identity.

- **Cross**: Your children will be marked with the sign of the cross sometimes with oil. This is to remind us all that your children are precious in the sight of God and protected by the love of Jesus Christ. Your children will be marked for ever as followers of the way of Jesus.

- **Water**: The water we pour during the service reminds us of many things. It reminds us that God's love is the source of life and will always be there. It also reminds us of God's grace, which forgives us and lets us make a new start when we fail to live up to our standards and God's standards.

- **Candle**: With Jesus as part of their lives, your children will never walk in darkness, but will have the light of life. They will take that light with them as they carry their candles out of church and for the rest of their lives. Their baptism candles are there to remind them that they are to shine as a light for others, and also that the light of God's love will never leave them.

- **Cheque book**: This may raise a laugh – and you may have to explain what it is! But a cheque book is a promise by one person to another and during the service there will some really important promises made. The next activity looks at those promises in more detail.

8. DECISIONS AND PROMISES (10 MINS)

You will need:

- A mirror.

- A calendar.

- Key words from the promises on large pieces of paper: pray, walk with them, care, help, church.

Very important promises are made in a baptism service. Important decisions are made too. Talk about the difference between a promise and decision.

Hold up the mirror. A decision is when we choose to take action. Look in the mirror and think about simple choices or those times when we either literally or in our minds tell ourselves we are going to do something. This is a decision.

Hold up the calendar. A promise is something we are going to do. It may happen every day, or it may happen on a specific day. Ask people to share examples of easy and difficult promises, or simple and serious ones.

Explain that the service involves both decisions and promises, some made to the child, some for the child, and some for ourselves.

Churches often worry about whether people understand enough about what these promises mean and what families are committing themselves to. However, parents and godparents may be less concerned about having an intellectual understanding of the words they are saying. For them, the most important aspect of these promises is their commitment to do the very best for the child and to give them a good start in life.

Invite the families to think about promises they have made in their lives. For example, they might include marriage vows, Brownie or Cub promises, taking an oath in a court, the military oath of allegiance, or promises to repay a debt or do a job.

In the baptism service, parents, godparents and the congregation make some very important promises. Read through the promises and decisions that will be in the service in your church.

You could pick out some of the key words and invite people to ask questions about them if they wish.

9. THE WAY WE DO THINGS HERE ... (15 MINS, OR SEPARATE REHEARSAL IN CHURCH)

It is very important for families to have a clear idea of what will happen during the service, and particularly what they will be expected to do and say. They are likely to be more relaxed and engage fully at the service if they are not worried about what is going to happen next.

Give each family a copy of your church's order of service, or put up an outline of it on a screen or flipchart.

- Make sure the families know that they don't need to remember anything – the person leading the service will always make sure they are in the right place and know what to do.

- Assure them that you and the congregation are going to be delighted to welcome the whole family to the service, including any children, and that you are relaxed about children and their parents doing whatever they need to do to make the service a relaxed and happy occasion. Give details of any special provision your church has for children, including the practicalities like toilets.

- Go through the order of service, drawing attention to the key elements that you covered in the previous activity. Make sure the parents are relaxed about where to sit, when to stand, when they will move to the front, etc, and any words they have to say. Stress again that you will be there to help.

- Invite questions.

10. TOOLS FOR THE JOURNEY (10 MINS)

Company

The journey that begins at baptism is not made alone. It is made in the company of others who can help and encourage on the way: family, friends and godparents; and the church family and friends.

Building and keeping relationships is really important, and is part of the amazing journey of faith. Just being together helps to grow strong relationships and helps children to discover more about other people. Discovery and imagination are part of what makes us unique humans. Wondering together at God's incredible world, laughing at fun things and learning how to get over mistakes are all important aspects of life after the christening.

- Pick up the idea from the opening activity about the things families enjoy doing. Look at the images and think about how many are simply about spending time together, creating special memories.

- Invite people to use their left hand to name five things they might enjoy doing indoors to build family relationships, for example: cooking, storytelling, craft activities, collecting.

- Invite people to use their right hand to name five things they might enjoy doing outdoors to build relationships, for example: gardening, taking a walk, swimming, going to a new place.

- Remind people that God is with them in all the ordinary things of life, good times and the hard times. That is part of the ongoing journey of faith.

- Light a candle and make the link to the candle that will be given at the baptism, reminding them that their child is a light for Jesus wherever they go, and that wherever they go Jesus will be a light for them.

- Explain that there are suggestions of things to do together on the website at **www.churchofenglandchristenings.org/after-a-christening/days-fun-times**.

Church family and friends

You will need: some invitation cards to an event like a party or celebration.

Background for session leaders: Families often say that they would like to have more contact with the church after their child's baptism. During the service, the congregation promises to welcome and uphold the candidate in their new life in Christ, and in baptism the child is welcomed as part of God's family. The people at church are all on the same journey of faith.

However, many parents have anxieties about coming to church, so this is a good time to talk about the whole breadth of church life with the families: toddler groups, coffee mornings, Messy Church, all-age worship, seasonal special events. If possible, invite a couple of people from the church to talk briefly about how they are involved and what it means to them.

Hand out the invitations and talk about how people feel when they have been invited to something. Talk about the difference between being invited and being a gatecrasher.

Explain that baptism means that they can never be gatecrashers at any church event, anywhere. They are always invited and welcome. If appropriate, talk about different churches they might go to – for example, when they are on holiday, or a well-known large church or cathedral such as Westminster Abbey.

9. DIRECTIONS AND HELP (10 MINS)

You will need:

- Map of your community that can be opened up on the floor or a large piece of paper.
- Sticky notes.
- Pens or pencils.
- An assortment of Bibles.

Once we are on a journey, especially one that lasts a lifetime, we need some sense of direction, and we might also need help and encouragement to keep us going. Families who are bringing a child for baptism will want to help their child to make good choices in life and may well appreciate Christian values and ethics, so discovering the tools that will help support the journey is important.

Direction and help for Christians can be found in lots of different ways – through conversations with others on the journey, through being in church, but also through reading the Bible and through praying.

Explain that there are many different ways of praying, just as there are many different ways of communicating with other people. Some prayers are written down in formal language; others may be shorter than a tweet. Some prayers do not use words at all, but are prayed through pictures, in music, or with our hearts and souls. There are no right or wrong words to use. Prayer is about spending time in God's company offering our thanks, worries, loved ones, or difficult situations into God's love and light, trusting in God's promise to hear us when we call upon him.

Praying for and with our children is one of the most important things we can do. In our prayers, we are treasuring them within the love and light of God, paying deep attention to the beauty and wonder of the people God created our children to be. This can be as simple as lighting a candle (see the christenings website **www.churchofenglandchristenings.org/light-candle-2**), or saying 'God, I pray for (*child's name*),' perhaps while looking at a photo of the child. There are more suggestions at **www.churchofenglandchristenings.org/ after-a-christening/prayer**.

Praying with children could include reading from books of children's prayers, saying a simple prayer together at bedtime, giving thanks before meals (saying grace) or saying the words, 'May God bless you and keep you,' to your child whenever you say goodbye. As children grow older, you could invite them to add their own words when you pray. It is worth keeping a notebook in the place where you pray to record things your child says that you want to remember.

Either lay out the map of your community, or invite people to call out places in your community that might be important in their child's life while you make a list: home, nursery, childminder, doctor's surgery, school, playground, hospital, play attraction, friend's house, and so on.

Ask everyone to write the name of their child on a sticky note. Walk round the map together, or look at the lists, and invite people to place their sticky note on a place that is important to their child.

Invite people to think quietly about what they might want to say to God while their child is in that particular place. It might, for example, begin, 'Thank you, God, for …' or, 'Please, God, take care of my child while …' Ask if anyone is happy to share their prayer.

10. SHARING GOD'S STORY (10 MINS)

You will need:

- Some family Bible resources, e.g. storybooks, children's Bibles, sticker books, books of puzzles and activities, DVDs, list of internet resources.

- Sticky dots or stars.

When people set off on a journey they often take maps, guidebooks, apps and other information to help them find their way around and to make the most of what they are doing. For Christians the Bible is the guidebook.

The Bible is the most read book in the world. It might surprise people how familiar certain stories or phrases from the Bible are. You might use the following or a similar list for a discussion, or as the basis of a quiz, but it is important not to make people feel stupid or ignorant.

- Art – maybe a picture of Leonardo da Vinci's *Last Supper* or Rembrandt's *Prodigal Son* (you can easily find these online and could show images).

- Film – *Prince of Egypt.*

- Music – *Joseph and the Amazing Technicolor Dreamcoat.*

- In school/nursery – Noah's ark.

- Everyday culture – nativity scene at Christmas or a cross on a public memorial.

- Everyday phrases – 'He thinks he can walk on water'; 'It was like David and Goliath'.

You might ask the group for other ideas.

Christians read the Bible to help them with everyday life. Explain that the Bible is not a single book. It contains 66 books in different styles: some are poetry, some history, others are letters.

The Bible includes stories, histories, poetry, guidance on good ways to live, letters, warnings, promises and dreams. It is the story of God's involvement with people, how people respond to God and how they learn to live with one another. It includes the story of Jesus, all that he did and said, his birth, death and resurrection. Christians find it encouraging and challenging.

Explain that many resources are available for families that will help them find out more about the contents of the Bible. Look through the collection you have brought. If you have a local Christian bookshop, they may be happy to organize a display of items on a 'sale or return' basis. You may want to buy something appropriate for each family.

If you have time, you might like to give each family a copy of part of Psalm 139, or a similar psalm, to take away, perhaps from a contemporary translation.

Read that psalm aloud as an example of how the Bible can help express deep thoughts and feelings.

11. CLOSING PRAYER

Prayer activity using oil, water and light

You will need:

- A cloth.

- A bottle of olive oil or a church oil stock.

- A bowl (ideally a clear one).

- A bottle of water.

- A candle and matches or a lighter (make sure it is in a suitable candle holder or on a heatproof mat).

Spread out the cloth, saying:

As we spread out this cloth, we bring to God all our hopes and dreams,
all our fears and worries.

Put the container of oil on the cloth, saying:

As we bring oil for healing and holiness, we ask God to bless our children,
our families, and our homes.

Put the bowl on the cloth, pour in the water, saying:

As we bring water for refreshment and cleansing, we ask God to fill us with
his love and his life.

Put the candle on the cloth and light it, saying:

As we bring light to show us the way, we ask God to show us how to help our
children to live well.

*Spend a few moments in quiet, looking at the items. Draw the time of prayer to
a close by using one of the following prayers, together if appropriate.*

The suggested prayers from the website **www.churchofenglandchristenings.
org/prayers**.

Creator God,

We thank you for the gift of the life of (*names of children*) who are to be baptized.

May your blessing of peace and joy be with them and protect them all of their days.

We make this prayer in the name of your Son, Jesus.

Amen.

You could give each family a magnet (available from **www.churchprinthub. org**) and suggest that they use it as a reminder to pray in the days leading up to the christening. Make sure you invite and encourage them to come along to church before the day to meet those people who will be praying for them in the days ahead.

AND FINALLY ...

As they leave the session, our hope and prayer is that the families will feel better prepared for their child's christening and that they will be beginning to discover that baptism is more than a one-off event.

We hope that you have enjoyed getting to know the families and have built relationships with them that will continue to grow and deepen at the children's baptism services and in the years to come. It is important to keep them in your prayers and to keep in touch with them.

SINGLE SESSION WITH ONE FAMILY

Some churches may find it difficult to get a group of families together for baptism preparation — perhaps your church only baptizes a few children each year, or you may not have a suitable meeting space. If this is the case, you are likely to meet the families one at a time. It can be helpful to visit them in their own homes, and you may think that this is easier for them. However, I have learned from experience that families sometimes feel anxious about welcoming the vicar into their living room. They often make sure everything is spotlessly clean and unnaturally tidy.

It may be better to offer families a choice, explaining that you can meet them in their home, or they could come to the church or your home if they prefer. I also ask them whether they would like anyone else to come along, such as godparents or grandparents. However, even if the usual way of doing baptism preparation is in a single session with one family, it's a great idea to encourage and invite them along to church. Many people have no idea what a church service might be like, or even that it is something that other people in the community are involved with. And it's really important for the family to meet people and begin to make friends.

When meeting a single family at home, in your own home or in a church building, there is less scope to offer creative activities, so this session suggests a very simple visual aid that can be used to help families remember the things you talked about. With only one family, the conversation can focus on their particular situation and questions. *Suggested visual aid*: bag or box of children's building blocks (you could use the family's own).

1. OPENING (5 MINS)

It would be good to begin the meeting by congratulating the family on deciding to have their child christened. A christening is a very special event and it's important to emphasize that you and the church want to do all you can to make it as special as possible. The material in this overview will take about an hour, but you may wish to spend longer with the family, getting to know them better. You could talk about such things as how they felt when they first saw their child, and the joys and the fears that come with responsibility and love.

Explain what you are going to cover during the meeting: the preparations for the child's christening, the day itself, and the difference baptism can make in the months and years ahead.

Explain that the words 'christening' and 'baptism' refer to the same special event in a child's life. Christening is a traditional word to describe the fact that the child will be welcomed as a member of the church. Baptism is the word used more often in churches. It means to be dipped or immersed and refers to the way water is used in the church service.

2. WHY ARE WE HERE? (5–10 MINS)

Begin by taking a few of the building blocks and ask the parents what made them decide to have their child baptized. Encourage them to think over what was important for them in their own childhood, what they hope the baptism will mean for their child, and for each reason lay down a brick.

Highlight the fact that many families think it is important for their children to have godparents and this is one of the reasons they give for wanting a christening. Godparents are a very significant part of the baptism service and can have a valuable role in their godchildren's lives over the years ahead. This leads us to the next section.

CORE PROGRAMME OVERVIEW: SINGLE SESSION WITH ONE FAMILY

Opening	5 minutes
Why are we here?	5–10 minutes
Godparents	10–15 minutes
Packing for a journey	10–15 minutes
Promises, promises	10 minutes
What will happen in the service	15 minutes (or separate rehearsal at church)
Carrying on the journey	10 minutes
	65–75 minutes

3. GODPARENTS (10–15 MINS)

Talk about the people who are going to be influential in the child's life in the years ahead, placing bricks for different groups of people like grandparents, siblings, aunts and uncles. When you mention godparents, pause and give them a row of bricks to themselves.

Godparents are very important. Parents often think very carefully before choosing people they trust to take a special interest in their child, act as good role models and play an important part in the life of the family. Ask why the godparents they have chosen are important to them and acknowledge the importance of lifetime friendships. A godparent is going to be part of a child's life for many, many years.

Churches also take the role of godparents very seriously, which is why there are some rules and guidelines about who can be a godparent when a child is baptized. You can find advice about this at **www. churchofenglandchristenings.org/for-parents/choosing-godparents**.

It is good practice for churches to make the requirements clear at a very early stage of the enquiry, so that families are aware of them before this preparation session. This is a good opportunity to check whether the family has any questions.

In particular, it may be worth checking that the people they have in mind do meet these requirements.

It is also worth making sure that people understand the difference between godparents and legal guardians. There is widespread confusion about the role of godparents if anything should happen to the child's parents. Being a godparent is not the same as being a legal guardian. It may be helpful to point out that if families choose as godparents people they would like to take care of their children should the need arise, they should also appoint them as legal guardians in their wills.

4. PACKING FOR A JOURNEY (10–15 MINS)

You can simply continue using bricks or you might like to add the following:

- A child's bag.

- The following items: map and/or guidebook; Bible; photograph of a group of friends; small cross and a name badge; and the oil that will be used in the service (if appropriate); bottle of water; torch; a candle like the ones you give to baptism families. N.B. If the session is in church, you could put each item in the appropriate place (as indicated in brackets), and walk from place to place to talk about each item and put it in the bag.

Talk about the challenge of packing for a holiday or a long journey, and all the kit that needs to be taken: the younger the child, the more equipment they need!

Explain that the service in which their child will be baptized is a way of packing some of the things their child will need on their journey through life as a follower of Jesus.

Either place a brick for each item as you talk or take the items mentioned and place in the bag.

- **Map, guidebook and Bible** (the place where people stand to read from the Bible, e.g. a lectern): We need directions to help us find the right path, and guidebooks give us interesting information about the places we visit. The Bible is a map and a guidebook to help us live a Christian way of life. Explain that there is a reading from the Bible in the service. Chat about the Bible and whether they have a Bible for their child, perhaps suggesting that it makes a good christening gift. *Place the map, guidebook and Bible in the bag.*

- **Photograph of a group of friends** (the place where the presentation of candidates takes place, e.g. the chancel step or by the font): When we go on a long journey, it's good to travel with friends – people we can share the experience with and remember it afterwards, to have fun with and to help us if we get into trouble. Talk about the people who will be at the child's christening service alongside the parents. These are the travelling companions:

  o **The godparents**, who will make a public commitment to support the child as they grow up and to help them live a Christian life.

  o **Other family and friends**, who will have gathered together to share this special day and will continue to care about you and your child.

  o **The church congregation** (or their representatives if the baptism takes place outside the main service), who will welcome your child as a new member of our community. They will also make a commitment to support the child and its parents and godparents. *Place another brick or put the photo in the bag.*

- **Cross and name badge**: (also at the chancel step/font). Talk about how on school trips and with big groups we are often given a name badge giving details of the group we belong to, as well as our name. During the service the child will be marked with the sign of the cross, which is a sign that they now belong to God's family and are surrounded by God's love.

Place another brick or put the cross and badge in the bag.

- *If you will use oil* **Sun cream and oil**: If our journey takes our family to sunny places, we make sure our children are covered in sun cream to protect their skin. In the service, the child will be marked with oil as a symbol of preparing them for the new way of life that begins at baptism. The priest will use the oil to make the sign of the cross as a symbol of God's protective love for the child. The oil actually represents many things – it's very difficult to think of anything that means quite the same in our ordinary life. As well as protecting the child, the oil helps us to pay attention to everything that is holy and special about them as a completely unique individual with their own gifts and their own beauty. You might use this moment to talk about the family's hopes and dreams for their child, but the oil is a sign that God has a special plan and a purpose. When the Queen was anointed with oil in her coronation service, it was such a special, holy moment, that the cameras were not allowed to film it. *Place another brick or put the sun cream and the oil in the bag.*

- **Water** (font): Talk about basic needs on the journey – food and drink. Water is one of the most basic and important things we need in life. It keeps us alive when we drink it, and we use it to keep ourselves clean and to refresh us. The water in the font reminds us of all these things. It also represents the idea that, at the moment of baptism, we are moving through the water from one way of life to another, just as we pass through the waters that break when we are born. We pass through the water as people in the Bible passed through the waters of the Red Sea on their way from slavery to freedom, and as Jesus passed through the waters of death and rose to new life. We also leave behind an old way of life when we are baptized; something dies and we rise to a new way of life in Christ. You may want to talk about the mistakes that we all make in life, the times we fall short of what we want to be or to do, and how the water reminds us that there is always forgiveness when we turn back to God.

Place another brick or put the water in the bag.

- **Torch and candle** (the place where candidates are given a candle, e.g. the chancel step or by the Easter candle): We need light for our journey. At night, we might put on our headlights or use a torch. If we wake up in the night feeling scared, perhaps because we have heard a strange noise, we are likely to turn on a light as soon as we can. Jesus said that he is the light of the world. Those who believe in him will never walk in darkness, but will have the light of life. However dark or difficult life is, we carry the light of Christ with us and it can show us the way forward. At the end of the service, the child will be given a candle to remind them that they carry the light of Christ with them for the rest of their lives. Talk about how children can be a sign of light in our lives, and also about how whatever they face in the years ahead the light will be with them. *Place another brick or put the torch and candle in the bag.*

Review the items that have been placed in the bag. Or look at the bricks on the structure you have been building, which should have a few rows now. Talk about how it's beginning to look like foundations for a building. The baptism is a foundation for the child's life ahead. Talk about the kind of values and beliefs that they see as a foundation to life and explain that the christening is the beginning of all this. It starts with some key decisions and promises made in the service.

5. PROMISES, PROMISES (10 MINS)

Very important promises are made in a baptism service.

Churches often worry about whether people understand enough about what these promises mean and what families are committing themselves to. However, parents and godparents may be less concerned about having an intellectual understanding of the words they are saying. For them, the most important aspect of these promises is their commitment to do the very best for the child and to give them a good start in life.

Invite the family to talk about other decisions and promises they have made in their lives. For example, they might include marriage vows, Brownie or Cub promises, taking an oath in a court, the military oath of allegiance, or promises to repay a debt or do a job.

In the baptism service, parents, godparents and the congregation make some very important promises. Read through the promises together. Place some more bricks on the structure to represent the big words of the promises, like pray, help, care, guide.

6. WHAT WILL HAPPEN IN THE SERVICE? (15 MINS)

Families are often anxious that they might not 'get things right'. As long as someone has run through the service with them, they are likely to be satisfied with even a small amount of baptism preparation. If at all possible, try to arrange to meet the family at church for a rehearsal where you can go through the mechanics of your building and allay fears about where to stand, what to say, when to move and so on.

During this visit, put their minds at ease and answer any practical questions they may have.

Give the family a copy of your church's order of service.

- Make sure the family knows that they don't need to remember anything – the person leading the service will always make sure they are in the right place and know what to do.

- Assure them that you and the congregation are going to be delighted to welcome the whole family to the service, including the children, and that you are relaxed about children and their parents doing whatever they need to do to make the service a relaxed and happy occasion.

- Go through the order of service, drawing attention to the key elements you covered earlier, and make sure they have time to ask questions.

7. CARRYING ON THE JOURNEY? (10 MINS)

In the family

Talk about how the christening day is the beginning of a journey and that there are lots of things that will help as they continue onwards, having given their child a good start.

Each of the following could be represented by a brick on the structure: people, the church, and prayer and Bible reading.

7a People

It's important to build relationships as family and with godparents. Explain that whether you are a parent or godparent, friend or relative, spending time with children you know can be really special, and it's part of the amazing journey of faith. Just being together helps to grow strong relationships and helps children to discover more about other people. Discovery and imagination are part of what makes us unique humans. Wondering together at God's incredible world, laughing at fun things and learning how to get over mistakes are all important aspects of life after the christening. It may be that there are memories to share already. You might like to show them the website where there are suggestions of things to do together (**www.churchofenglandchristenings.org/after-a-christening/days-fun-times**).

7b The church

Talk about how during the service the congregation makes promises to welcome and support the child in their new life in Christ. The child is now part of God's family, and wherever they go, now and in the future, they will always find a welcome and a place.

Explain how your local church supports families, not just through Sunday services but in other ways, from coffee mornings to toddler groups. Research shows that often parents want to come back to church, but are anxious about expectations of commitment and worried about whether it's appropriate for young children. However, families may well return at times of special celebrations around Christmas or Harvest – and to something like a summer fete, where there are child-friendly activities and a chance to meet people in a relaxed way.

Simply coming to a church fair or coffee morning may be a daunting step for some families. If they feel warmly welcomed and are invited to other events, these small steps can become significant in a family's spiritual journey. Talk to the family about what might interest them, and make sure you have their contact details for the future.

7c Prayer and Bible reading

Many parents will already be praying for their child in some way. Explain that there are many different ways of praying with a child. There are no right or wrong words to use. Prayer is about spending time in God's company offering our thanks, worries, loved ones, or difficult situations into God's love and light, trusting in God's promise to hear us when we call upon him.

Praying for and with our children is one of the most important things we can do. This can be as simple as lighting a candle (see the christenings website **www.churchofenglandchristenings.org/light-candle-2**), or saying, 'God, I pray for (*child's name*),' perhaps while looking at a photo of the child. If they have a night light, you could pray for the child as you turn it on, that they will be a light for others in their life. There are other suggestions at **www.churchofenglandchristenings.org/after-a-christening/prayer**.

7d Sharing God's story

Take a few moments to talk about the Bible and where to start sharing it with children. Many parents value ideas and suggestions as to which stories to tell or which version of the Bible to buy. There are now lots of interactive games and online resources that can help even very young children discover some of the stories that have not only shaped our culture and history but will also shape our lives.

Before you draw the conversation to a close, recap the main things that you have said.

Having a child baptized at a christening is a great start to an amazing journey of faith that will last a lifetime. Parents, godparents and the wider church will be there for the child and the family in the years ahead. Prayer, the Bible and discovering God in creation and worship are all delights to uncover.

End the time by introducing a simple prayer.

8. CLOSING PRAYER (5 MINS)

You might like to light a candle.

Suggested prayer from the website **www.churchofenglandchristenings.org/ prayers**.

Creator God,

We thank you for the gift of the life of (*name of child*) who is to be baptized. May your blessing of peace and joy be with them and protect them all of their days.

We make this prayer in the name of your Son, Jesus.

Amen.

AND FINALLY ...

By the time the session ends, our hope and prayer is that the family feel prepared for their child's christening and will be beginning to discover that baptism is more than a one-off event.

We hope that you have enjoyed getting to know the family and have built a relationship with them that will continue to grow and deepen at the child(ren)'s baptism services and in the years to come. It is important to keep them in your prayers and to keep in touch with them.

For further information:

www.churchofenglandchristenings.org

www.churchsupporthub.org

www.churchprinthub.org

STARTING RITE

Spiritual nurture for babies and their parents

When Anglican priest Jenny Paddison became a mother, there were numerous activities for new parents and their babies on offer: baby yoga, baby massage, baby swimming – but nothing from the church. In response, she created this five session programme that connects with the immense sense of wonder and joy that new parents experience and provides spiritual nurture from the outset, recognising the innate capacity for spirituality with which we are born.

Starting Rite is designed specifically for babies up to a year old and their parents. It provides a complete practical companion to offering the programme locally, including story scripts, simple songs, ideas for multi-sensory play, as well as lists of equipment needed and how to create a welcoming atmosphere. It explores Christian themes though activities like peek-a-boo, blowing bubbles and splashing in water.

Starting Rite enables local churches to offer a welcome to all new parents, and can also be used as a baptism preparation course.

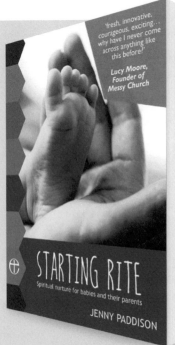

'fresh, innovative, courageous, exciting... why have I never come across anything like this before?'

Lucy Moore,
Founder of
Messy Church

STARTING RITE
Spiritual nurture for babies and their parents

JENNY PADDISON

978 0 7151 4726 9   £19.99

www.chpublishing.co.uk

CHURCH HOUSE PUBLISHING